PRAISE FOR *ROCK-SOLID TEACHER*

There is no better model of teaching for results than that of our
Lord Jesus Christ while He was on this Earth. Greg Carlson, a good friend
and colleague, has spent many years developing and teaching others the
principles within this book. Anyone can apply these principles and
become a better teacher almost immediately.

JACK EGGAR
PRESIDENT AND CEO
AWANA CLUBS INTERNATIONAL

Rock-Solid Teacher defines "master teacher" like no other because it thoroughly
unveils the teaching principles and methods of the true Master Teacher.
My good friend and co-worker, Dr. Greg Carlson, has spent a lifetime
studying, understanding and imitating Jesus' teaching, and it shows in this
book that is balanced with deep insights and practical applications. This is
Greg's life message, and through it God has used him to influence thousands
of others to teach as Jesus taught. This incredible book will leave you with a
profound appreciation for Jesus' teaching and a deep desire to be an imitator
of Christ—not only in your daily walk, but also in your teaching!

LARRY FOWLER
EXECUTIVE DIRECTOR OF GLOBAL TRAINING
AWANA CLUBS INTERNATIONAL

Sadly, in some circles, the goal of teaching means turning simple ideas
into complicated ones, so that only a few can understand. Jesus, the
Master Teacher, never knew such nonsense, as *Rock-Solid Teacher* explains.
Dr. Gregory Carlson skillfully outlines a handful of simple core
principles from our Lord's ministry that will empower both novice
and experienced teachers alike. Don't miss this gem!

RONALD T. HABERMAS, PH.D.
MCGEE PROFESSOR OF BIBLICAL STUDIES AND CHRISTIAN FORMATION
JOHN BROWN UNIVERSITY
SILOAM SPRINGS, ARKANSAS

Everyone believes that Jesus was the greatest teacher, but here is a book that
shows us how His methods can be ours. Here is practical help for all of us who
want to improve our teaching skills and learn from our Master.

DR. ERWIN W. LUTZER
SENIOR PASTOR, THE MOODY CHURCH
CHICAGO, ILLINOIS

ROCK SOLID TEACHER

Gregory C. Carlson

Gospel Light

Ventura, California, U.S.A.

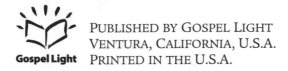

PUBLISHED BY GOSPEL LIGHT
VENTURA, CALIFORNIA, U.S.A.
PRINTED IN THE U.S.A.

Gospel Light is a Christian publisher dedicated to serving the local church. We believe God's vision for Gospel Light is to provide church leaders with biblical, user-friendly materials that will help them evangelize, disciple and minister to children, youth and families.

It is our prayer that this Gospel Light book will help you discover biblical truth for your own life and help you meet the needs of others. May God richly bless you.

For a free catalog of resources from Gospel Light, please call your Christian supplier or contact us at 1-800-4-GOSPEL *or* www.gospellight.com.

Cover image © Lars Justinen / GoodSalt.com

Library of Congress Cataloging-in-Publication Data
Carlson, Gregory C.
  Rock-solid teacher / Gregory C. Carlson.
    p. cm.
  Includes bibliographical references.
  ISBN 0-8307-3920-3 (hard cover)
  1. Christian education. 2. Teaching—Religious aspects—Christianity. 3. Education—Aims and objectives. I. Title.
BV1464.C37 2006
268'.6—dc22   2006015492

1   2   3   4   5   6   7   8   9   10   /   10   09   08   07   06

Rights for publishing this book in other languages are contracted by Gospel Light Worldwide, the international nonprofit ministry of Gospel Light. Gospel Light Worldwide also provides publishing and technical assistance to international publishers dedicated to producing Sunday School and Vacation Bible School curricula and books in the languages of the world. For additional information, visit www.gospellightworldwide.org; write to Gospel Light Worldwide, P.O. Box 3875, Ventura, CA 93006; or send an e-mail to info@gospellightworldwide.org.

CONTENTS

ROCK-SOLID TEACHERS:
FOLLOW
THE MASTER'S
EXAMPLE

I once attended a teaching principle seminar where the presenter was a nationally admired teacher. I won't name the individual, but my own respect for his teaching was so great that for weeks I eagerly anticipated watching and learning from his creative approaches and solid Bible teaching.

When the weekend of the conference finally arrived, I arrived early at the hotel meeting room and took a seat at a table with a number of other equally excited participants. We all opened our professionally prepared notebooks and got ready to be wowed. Instead, we spent eight hours listening to the speaker lecture, tell a few slightly amusing stories, and scroll through some nice PowerPoint slides.

Extremely disappointed, I made my way back to my hotel room, wishing I'd saved the organization I work for all that money I'd spent on the seminar.

Later, I realized what was missing. Yes, the speaker shared the promised teaching principles. Sure, the material was all professionally prepared. But the speaker neglected to incorporate the outstanding experiences that Jesus used to teach His disciples, His other followers, people who had never heard of Him, and even His enemies.

My experience made me want to be a better teacher—a *rock-solid teacher*—whether I was teaching a third-grade Sunday School class, leading a group of teenagers in a youth ministry Bible study, or training Christian education professionals with Awana Clubs International, where I work.

What Is a Rock-Solid Teacher?

A rock-solid teacher follows the Master Teacher's example. Of course, the Master Teacher is Jesus! He defined rock-solid teaching. Who had more compassion and better wisdom about people? "He knew all men," reported the apostle John (John 2:24). He had a grasp of God's Word, for He was and is the Word (see John 1:1). And as for changing people's lives, the heart of every believer is the result of Jesus' teaching.

Jesus epitomizes the definition of Bible teaching: one hand on the student, the other on the Word of God, bringing them together for life change. When we teach, we must have a grasp of the needs of our students. And certainly we want to grasp the meaning of the Scriptures. But the real skill and art of teaching is leading our students to life change!

One hand
on the
students

The other hand
on the
Word of God

Bringing them
together
for Life Change

Teaching Approaches

This definition of teaching describes three basic orientations or approaches to teaching: student orientation, subject orientation, and style orientation.

Student Orientation

Some approach the ministry of teaching with their relationship with the student in view. This is usually the case with parents. Many youth leaders also demonstrate this amazing ability at rapport.

These teachers approach the learning task by asking the question, "*Who* am I teaching?"

Subject Orientation

Another group approaches teaching ministry with a subject focus. They want to know the facts, outline what a passage says and means, and communicate content to their students.

These teachers approach the instruction time by asking, *"What* am I teaching?"

Style Orientation

Still others approach teaching with the goal of developing interaction, understanding and change in the student's life. They understand their role as a teacher and that the learning process involves integration of new teaching forms and methods.

These teachers approach a lesson by asking, *"How* am I going to teach?"

The Goal of Rock-Solid Teachers

To be master teachers, I believe we have to develop all three orientations. That's the goal of this book—to help you develop and improve your teaching skills by observing what Jesus did, establishing wise principles of teaching, and putting the principles into practice with some sound and practical methods.

This threefold course of action follows an effective pattern for teaching that is outlined in Scripture:

From the passage;
To the principle;
Toward the practice.

Chapter 1 looks at the overall job description of a master teacher. God calls us to proclaim truth, interact in teaching, and heal. Practice with skills used in evangelism highlights this threefold ministry of rock-solid teachers.

Chapters 2 through 4 provide an in-depth look at each aspect of the teaching ministry. The skills of lecturing, storytelling, question-asking and relationship-building enable teachers to move toward creative and effective teaching in their own ministries.

Chapter 5 explores the learning experiences and activities that Jesus used when teaching His disciples, and helps teachers integrate these principles into their classrooms and meetings.

Chapter 6 looks at the important aspect of understanding the students' needs and motivating them to learn.

Chapter 7 focuses on strengthening the teacher's grip on the Word of God, emphasizing the balance between content and molding students' lives through appropriate learning experiences.

Chapter 8 explores the learning environment. The master teacher will use setting and environment to ensure that maximum learning takes place.

Chapter 9 describes the outcome of rock-solid teaching: becoming like Jesus Christ! Master teachers understand the priority of an intense and satisfying relationship with the Lord through prayer.

Happy reading! Profound pondering! Rock-solid teaching! Go for it!

CHAPTER 1

TEACH LIKE JESUS!

Key Idea: Rock-solid teachers follow Jesus' model of proclaiming, instructing and healing.

Jesus went throughout Galilee, teaching in their synagogues, preaching the good news of the kingdom, and healing every disease and sickness among the people.

MATTHEW 4:23

During my Bible college days, I traveled with a musical group representing the school. A professor who was a wonderful communicator traveled with us. Whether he was holding a group of young people in the grip of his words or explaining a Bible passage in the van as we traveled, the truth of Scripture came alive when he spoke. He was a master teacher proclaiming truth.

This professor also created fantastic interaction in his Christian education classes. He urged students to think, integrate, apply and wrestle with the truth. Camaraderie developed among the students as we listened to his stories and asked and answered questions. The insights I gained made the difficult youth ministry that I was leading start to make sense. This professor was a master teacher instructing truth.

When I got married, I remember nervously inquiring if this professor and his wife could travel to Kansas to perform the wedding ceremony in my fiancée's church. He consented, but only on the condition that my soon-to-be-wife, Donna, and I went through premarital counseling with him. During those sessions, I was lifted to a place of learning about marriage. I found some areas that needed to be mended. When the day of our wedding arrived, I felt ready to joyously obey the Lord in loving and serving my wife. This professor was a master teacher who healed with truth.

I'm not sure I realized it back then, but the ways my professor taught me in these different situations followed the teaching style of Jesus: proclaiming truth, instructing in truth, and healing with truth.

As we look at fulfilling the overall job description of master teachers, we're also called to proclaim truth, interact in instruction, and bring healing. Let's briefly explore each of these areas by looking at Jesus' ministry, and examine how to use each area specifically when we evangelize. We can then list some practical ways to use proclaiming, instructing and healing in our teaching ministries. (In addition to this overview, chapter 2 will delve deeper into proclaiming, chapter 3 into instruction, and chapter 4 into healing and building relationships.)

Can I Really Teach Like Jesus?

Most of us wonder if we can possibly measure up to the way Jesus taught. Of course, Jesus could teach like a master: He was—and is—God! But instead of worrying about how we measure up, let's focus on the ways in which we can become more like Jesus. Some important truths to remember about Jesus' teaching ministry:

Jesus was fully human. Jesus' deity doesn't negate His humanity. Practically speaking, if Jesus taught in our present physical locations, He'd still have to prepare a lesson, set up His media projector, arrange chairs and turn on the lights. He'd have to explain to His teaching team why He wanted to try a new way of doing things. He'd have to deal with unmotivated students.

In other words, when Jesus taught, He had to deal with the same kind of limitations of preparation, presentation and response that we deal with today. Jesus was a normal guy. That's part of the reason why the people of His hometown found His teaching so amazing!

Jesus promised the Holy Spirit would fill and empower our teaching. What a promise! We can't live out Christ's way of teaching unless the Holy Spirit enables us with His presence. "When he, the Spirit of truth, comes, he will guide you into all truth. He will not speak on his own; he will speak only what he hears, and he will tell you what is yet to come. He will bring glory to me by taking from what is mine and making it known to you" (John 16:13-14).

Teacher of teachers Roy Zuck, who served as professor of Bible exposition at Dallas Seminary, states, "Christian teachers depend on the Spirit of God to enable them to do three things: (1) introduce their lessons in ways that will capture interest and that will relate to the problems, needs, and experiences of pupils—as Christ often did; (2) show how the Bible is relevant to pupils' experiences; and (3) lead pupils to see and appropriate the Word of the Lord as the answer to their personal needs."[1]

Jesus promised that we would do greater works than He did. "I tell you the truth, anyone who has faith in me will do what I have been doing. He will do even greater things than these, because I am going to the Father"

(John 14:12). Jesus didn't necessarily mean that we would do more miraculous works than He did, but that we could potentially reach students with spiritual change.

Becoming more like Jesus is a process. This holds true in the ways we grow spiritually as well as in the ways we learn to teach as Jesus did. During her college days, Donna traveled in a music group with Jane, an enthusiastic young Christian. But Jane grew frustrated because she wanted to be as mature as Donna, who'd grown up in a Christian home and came to know Christ in early childhood. Donna encouraged Jane to grow in the Lord one day at a time. Some 30 years later, Jane has indeed become a great mom, discipler and teacher. As author Bruce Wilkinson says, "Master teachers are not born, not manufactured, but just improved."[2]

Jesus developed like we do. Jesus had to grow, increase (see Luke 2:40,52), and learn (see Heb. 5:8). If Jesus had to develop, how much more should we encourage ourselves and others to develop in the things that are important?

I often tell evangelical teachers, "If something's worth doing, it's worth doing poorly *at first* until you can do it better!" Too many of us think that we have to be perfect in our teaching and forget that we should be developing toward excellence. As we develop, we'll never be perfect, but we can always give our first and best!

With the understanding that we can indeed become more like Jesus in our teaching, let's look in-depth at the model He provided.

Proclaiming as Jesus Proclaimed

Jesus certainly proclaimed! In his Gospel, Mark summarized the beginning of Jesus' ministry: "So he traveled throughout Galilee, preaching in their synagogues and driving out demons" (Mark 1:39).

Our English Bibles translate two Greek words as "preach" or "proclaim." One is *euangelizo,* from which we derive our English word "evangelical." *Euangelizo* means "to proclaim, declare, or show good tidings." The other word is *kerusso,* which means "to preach, proclaim, publish, or be a herald."[3] The idea behind both of these meanings is to get the listener to pay attention and respond. With response comes life change.

Jesus proclaimed the following truths:

- Repentance (see Matt. 4:17)
- The nearness of the kingdom of heaven (see Matt. 10:7)
- Authority over demons (see Mark 3:15)
- Good news (see Mark 16:15)
- The kingdom of God (see Luke 9:2)

Jesus also commissioned the disciples to proclaim: "He appointed twelve—designating them apostles—that they might be with him and that he might send them out to preach" (Mark 3:14). Notice that the disciples continually spent time in intimate fellowship *with* Jesus, learning from Him as He instructed and practiced various forms of ministry. Then, after the disciples learned from Jesus, they went out to preach.

As Jesus proclaimed truth, these highlights emerged:

- *Jesus always made the good news of the Kingdom a priority.* Even when Jesus didn't speak of salvation through faith directly, it was always a part of His proclamation.

- Jesus always expected a response when He proclaimed the truth. When Jesus ministered to people, He didn't allow passive neglect. He usually established a "dividing line" that called for people either to believe or to go their own way. The disciples left everything and followed, the Pharisees resisted, the scribes debated, the crowds wondered.

The children's club at our church usually ran like a fine-tuned machine. Yet at the end of the year, we realized that very few of our third-through sixth-grade students had responded to the message of the gospel. So, the next year, we intentionally had the ministry's group leaders emphasize the story of salvation to these students. As the ministry leaders taught with renewed purpose, many children began to trust in Christ and grow in their faith.

Do you proclaim truth with the students you teach? Do you make the gospel a priority? Do your students respond? At the end of this chapter, we'll look at some practical ways you can make sure your teaching ministry includes the aspect of proclaiming. But first, let's explore the way Jesus instructed.

Teaching as Jesus Taught

Have you ever asked a child about a Sunday School or club ministry lesson and heard him answer, "The teacher learned us . . ." While this phrase reflects bad English grammar, it actually comes quite close to the root meaning of the Greek word *didasko* ("teaching" in Matthew 4:23). It could be translated "to learn someone"! It's actually a great description of the way that Jesus taught. We might say that He caused His students to learn. But just what did that kind of teaching look like?

Jesus held forth truth. The chief priests and teachers of the Law unsuccessfully tried to trip up Jesus and question His authority. They even sent spies who pretended to be honest to question Jesus. The spies asked Jesus, "We know that you speak and teach what is right, and that you do not show partiality but teach the way of God in accordance with the truth" (Luke 20:21). We don't know if these individuals sincerely meant the compliment or were just saying what the crowd believed. Either way, their statement showed that Jesus spoke the truth.

Even this brief episode provides several guidelines that we can use in our teaching:

- Teach what's right.
- Don't show partiality.
- Teach the truth.

Jesus was willing to admonish. When a rich young man asked Jesus what he could do to earn eternal life, Jesus counseled him to obey the commandments (see Matt. 19:16-17). Jesus also provoked the young man to correct his belief about eternal life. The young man wanted to know what "good thing" he could do, but Jesus pointed out that no one could hope to be good enough to enter heaven.

As teachers, we can't admonish students to be perfect. But with God, "all things are possible" (Matt. 19:26). So, we can correct students to be obedient.

Holding forth truth and admonishing sound a lot like proclamation, don't they? Of course! There's overlap and similarity. We can't separate proclaiming and instructing from each other.

When I served as a pastor, one of my deacons once asked me, "Where does preaching end and teaching begin?" I responded that Jesus seemed to move seamlessly in His ministry between preaching and teaching based on the needs of the hearer and the nature of the learning situation.

Jesus modeled what He taught. Jesus encouraged imitation: "I have set you an example that you should do as I have done for you" (John 13:15). As teachers, we should become more like our Lord and encourage our students to do the same. However, we also need to remember that our students will often try to be like us. That's a weighty responsibility for teachers.

Jesus guided those He taught. Jesus guided His disciples when they needed new information. He corrected wrong beliefs, reproved errant behavior, and showed them the way toward right behavior by both modeling it and shaping the disciples to follow. When James and John, two brothers who were Jesus' disciples, asked for positions of prestige and power, Jesus corrected them. He pointed out that greatness wouldn't come from ruling with Him, but through serving others (see Mark 10:35-45).

Jesus used the concept of shepherding. Jesus said, "I am the good shepherd; I know my sheep and my sheep know me" (John 10:14). While we often think of pastors as shepherds and church members as sheep, teachers are shepherds too. This analogy provides a beautiful picture of the instruction of a teacher. As teachers, our role involves making sure our students (sheep) know the way to take. Yet often we expect students to choose and behave without really knowing the Lord's will.

Jesus prayed for those He taught. Just before Jesus was arrested and the events leading to His death played out, He spent time praying for Himself and for all who would eventually believe in Him. But He also spent time praying specifically for the disciples. Jesus dedicated them to the Father by praying for their future ministry without Him and for their protection (see John 17).

As teachers, we have the privilege to take our students' needs to the Lord. Imagine the changes that would occur in your students' lives if you consistently dedicated them to God and prayed for their protection, future service and ministry.

Jesus served those He taught. Do you recall the Last Supper? In John 13, as the disciples reclined to eat dinner, Jesus took a towel and washed their smelly and dirty feet, immediately providing an active example of a serving leader. Of course, the primary way that Jesus served us was to give His life as the payment for our sin. That was the ultimate act of service.

All the ways that Jesus taught called for a response from the student. When He taught, people responded in the following ways:

- *They were amazed.* "The people were amazed at his teaching, because he taught them as one who had authority, not as the teachers of the law" (Mark 1:22).

- *Crowds gathered to Him.* "Large crowds from Galilee, the Decapolis, Jerusalem, Judea and the region across the Jordan followed him" (Matt. 4:25).

- *They were paralyzed with wonder.* "The temple guards went back to the chief priests and Pharisees, who asked them, 'Why didn't you bring [Jesus] in?' 'No one ever spoke the way this man does,' the guards declared" (John 7:45-46).

Healing as Jesus Healed

Although we sometimes shy away from discussing healing because of confusion about the subject, the Bible is straightforward about the healing ministry of Jesus. The word "healing" in our English Bible comes from five Greek words (or seven, if you add the words for "save" that are sometimes translated "heal"). From these words, we can derive two primary meanings: (1) to serve as a caretaker; and (2) to cure. Both meanings have significance for our ministry as teachers.

Jesus as Caretaker

The caretaker dimension of Jesus' healing ministry has the following components:

Jesus served in His teaching/healing. Jesus cared for the needs of others. Often, we see the wonder of Jesus' healing ministry but miss the practical service that Jesus performed. Think of how He served when He miraculously fed the 5,000, when He cast out the demon from a young boy and restored him to his father, when He cleansed the lepers, when He gave sight to the blind, when He caused the lame to walk, and when He raised the dead. In all of these cases, Jesus met people's needs and prepared them to learn.

Jesus deepened perspectives in His teaching/healing. Jesus used physical healing to help the disciples expand their viewpoint of people. His disciples often had skewed perspectives that hindered their ministry. For example, in John 9:2-3, just before Jesus healed the blind man, His disciples asked Him, "Rabbi, who sinned, this man or his parents, that he was born blind?" Jesus replied, "Neither this man nor his parents sinned, but this happened so that the work of God might be displayed in his life."

While the common teaching of the day was that suffering was always caused by sin, Jesus changed the disciples' perspective. He pointed out that the blind man's suffering wasn't directly caused by his sin or his parents but existed so that God's great works could be seen. Jesus knew that He would heal the blind man's sight before the man was even born!

Jesus lifted through His teaching/healing. While others were enthralled that demons were being cast out in Jesus' name, Jesus had the priority of eternal life in mind: "Do not rejoice that the spirits submit to you, but rejoice that your names are written in heaven" (Luke 10:20). When Lazarus died and all Martha could see was the rotting corpse of her brother, Jesus grasped the glory of God: "Did I not tell you that if you believed, you would see the glory of God?" (John 11:40).

Do you see it? Jesus brought people into an audience with God through His healing ministry. Jesus met needs to place people before

God. So what about you? Are your students being ignored or prepared? Do they feel energized and primed to learn, or do they feel drained and pushed away?

Jesus as Curer

Often, the Gospels describe Jesus' healing to show the importance of salvation and spiritual growth (spiritual healing), repaired relationships and the mending of damaged emotions (inner healing), and how God uses physical ailments and restoration of health to bring awareness and receptivity to His work.

Spiritual healing of people. In Mark 2:6-12, Jesus tried to communicate this message to the Pharisees in the incident of the paralytic man let down through the roof:

> Now some teachers of the law were sitting there, thinking to themselves, "Why does this fellow talk like that? He's blaspheming! Who can forgive sins but God alone?"
>
> Immediately Jesus knew in his spirit that this was what they were thinking in their hearts, and he said to them, "Why are you thinking these things? Which is easier: to say to the paralytic, 'Your sins are forgiven,' or to say, 'Get up, take your mat and walk?' But that you may know that the Son of Man has authority on earth to forgive sins . . ." He said to the paralytic, "I tell you, get up, take your mat and go home." He got up, took his mat and walked out in full view of them all. This amazed everyone and they praised God, saying, "We have never seen anything like this!"

In other words, Jesus was saying that the spiritual dimension of an individual's life is so important that it doesn't compare with his or her physical health. In his Gospel, Matthew describes the spiritual healing that comes to a person via salvation: "For this people's heart has become calloused; they hardly hear with their ears, and they have closed their eyes. Otherwise they might see with their eyes, hear with their ears, understand with their hearts and turn, and I would heal them" (Matt.

13:15). We can also be spiritual healers in our teaching ministries.

Inner healing or wholeness of people. The writer of the book of Hebrews described how God provides an inner holiness through His sanctifying work: "Make level paths for your feet, so that the lame may not be disabled, but rather healed. Make every effort to live in peace with all men and to be holy; without holiness no one will see the Lord" (Heb. 12:13-14).

Inner healing results in sanctification and holiness. Jesus demonstrated how this holiness was manifested in the lives of people to whom He ministered:

- The Samaritan leper, who returned to thank Jesus for healing him (see Luke 17:16)
- Zacchaeus, who decided to pay restitution to anyone he had robbed (see Luke 19:8)
- The woman caught in adultery, who desired to leave her life of sin (see John 8:11)
- The man who had been an invalid for 38 years, who, without doubting Jesus, picked up his mat and walked away (see John 5:1-9)

Don't underestimate the power of the curative ministry of healing in your teaching! I've seen club leaders tame unruly kids by teaching about the peace of Christ. I know a teenager who has received strength through the consistent attention and application of truth that his small group modeled for him. Adults may appear to be self-sufficient, but underneath they hunger for an encouraging word from their teacher. Families have been restored through the faithful sharing of God's grace.

The physical healing of people. One of the main reasons Jesus performed miracles was to demonstrate that He was indeed God and that His ministry was valid. As word about Jesus' healing ministry spread through the region, people thronged to experience His healing touch. "News about him spread all over Syria, and people brought to him all who were ill with various diseases, those suffering severe pain, the demon-possessed, those having seizures, and the paralyzed, and he healed them" (Matt. 4:24).

As a junior in high school, I had a severe accident that damaged my right forearm. I spent a number of weeks in the hospital. My pastor and my dad both spent considerable time praying with me. They helped me to see what I should hold on to. As I healed, these two men nurtured a newfound openness to the Lord's work in my life. The physical healing and the miracle of being alive resulted in my passion to learn and serve God with my life.

Perhaps we'll never heal people like Jesus did. But as the Lord meets needs and prepares hearts, we as teachers can expect to see healing through our teaching ministry.

Using Jesus' Model of Teaching

We can use Jesus' model of proclaiming, teaching and healing in all aspects of our teaching ministries. But as an example of how His model works, let's apply it to the important area of evangelism.

Jesus set the example:

- *In proclaiming truth:* He used the Ten Commandments to guide seekers to Himself as the fulfillment of God's perfect demands. Jesus didn't hold back when He proclaimed truth. In fact, He fully expected people to respond.

- *In His teaching:* Jesus seemed to be ready at any point to start where a person was at to bring them to knowledge of Himself. He exhorted His disciples when they had sufficient evidence for their faith.

- *In His healing:* Jesus was tender and compassionate when someone was broken and contrite.

In your teaching ministry, how can you proclaim truth, instruct for life change and offer healing, specifically in the area of evangelism? Consider the following suggestions:

With Children

- *Proclaim*. Clarify what the gospel of grace is all about. One of the things I appreciate about Art Rorheim, one of the founders of Awana Clubs International, is that he keeps bringing people back to clarity of the central place of the gospel of grace. Art says, "Sometimes, we need to help people understand what the gospel is *not* as much as we need to train for what the gospel is."

  For example, we can train children's workers to make sure they don't confuse students by using language the children don't understand. Too often, we think that phrases such as "inviting Jesus into your heart" or "make a commitment to Christ" communicate to children. But we can't assume that they understand what we mean—even adults often get confused by these same phrases. It's better to share the gospel simply.[4]

- *Teach*. Evaluate how often you share the gospel in your teaching ministry. Sunday School used to be a place where many heard the gospel. But today, too few children come to the Lord through this ministry.

With Youth

- *Proclaim*. Prompt youth to live the gospel and share the gospel while in high school. Teenagers can share their own personal testimony. It doesn't have to be dramatic, just practical. They can share the gospel not only with their lifestyle, but also with a clear and simple presentation.

  "You never told me!" I heard those words from a high school friend after we'd gone to separate colleges for several years. We'd both returned to a homecoming football game, and my friend shared that he'd come to know the Lord as his Savior. "I always knew you were religious," he said, "but there was something different! Yet in all the years of junior high and high school, you never told me about how to know Jesus in a personal relationship." I always recalled this conversation as I taught and mentored youth groups in later years.

- *Heal.* Invite teenagers to pray both for their friends' salvation and for all the challenges of life. One youth group I led recognized that we needed to pray if we wanted God to use our evangelistic efforts. Almost a third of our youth meeting became small-group prayer time. We prayed for friends and their struggles and joys. We prayed for parents, teachers and bosses. We were amazed at how God answered our prayers as scores of people came to know Him.

With Adults

- *Proclaim.* Don't assume that all regular class members have trusted Christ for salvation. I once developed an evaluation sheet for a seminar our ministry was doing and included a response box that stated "as a result of today's seminar, I made a decision to trust Christ as my personal Savior." Some people wondered why we'd include this response, since we were teaching children's and youth ministry leaders from evangelical churches. But when the first round of surveys came in, we found that nearly every session had adults coming to faith.

- *Heal.* Make sure that new people in Sunday School classes or small groups feel welcome. Often, new people need warm fellowship to create the right environment for coming to know the Lord. I know of one church that has greeters in the parking lot to make sure that everyone hears a friendly hello.

With Families

- *Teach.* Equip newly saved children and teenagers to minister to unsaved members of their families.

1. Emphasize to children and teens that parents will be more open to participating in spiritual conversations when they see how a relationship with Christ has changed the child's life.

2. Equip the child or teen to explain their decision to their families in a non-condemning way. The Holy Spirit will change the parent's heart.

3. Offer support in the days and weeks following the witness to the person's family. Pray for and with the child or teen. Ask God to be at work in the parent's heart.

I once received a phone call from the mother of a girl in a youth group I led. The mom was concerned that her daughter wanted to throw away her birth-control pills now that she'd become a Christian. I listened, sought to understand the mother, encouraged communication between the mother and daughter, and tried to explain where the daughter might be coming from. The girl and I spent a lot of time in prayer as she lovingly sought to honor her mom and still honor God. Eventually, the mom recognized the positive changes in the character and actions of her daughter, and she later also became a strong believer.

With Your Own Family

• *Heal.* Determine to be a blessing to your community. My family has used these strategies:

1. We prayed for neighbors, friends of our sons, community acquaintances and others with whom we came into contact.

2. We joined with our church family to establish a "lighthouse" ministry. As we discovered opportunities with

our neighbors, we related to their needs for prayer or encouragement.

3. We made our home the place where kids in the neighborhood came to play and hang out. That meant having an unlimited supply of soda and snacks, staying alert for fun games to play, and not being concerned about the way the grass was worn down.

Self-Check

Before you turn to chapter 2, take a few minutes to evaluate how you're fulfilling your role as a rock-solid teacher. Just between you and God, rate how you're doing at proclaiming, instructing and healing. Spend some time in prayer asking God to help you grow in areas in which you're struggling.

Proclaiming
I regularly make the truths of the Scriptures known to students to allow them to hear and respond to Jesus.
strongly agree   *agree*   *not sure*   *disagree*   *strongly disagree*

I consistently declare the truths of God's Word—even the more difficult ones—so that my students desire to become more like Christ.
strongly agree   *agree*   *not sure*   *disagree*   *strongly disagree*

Instructing
I prompt interaction around Scripture during teaching times and also encourage students to search God's Word in their times of individual study.
strongly agree   *agree*   *not sure*   *disagree*   *strongly disagree*

I balance the many roles of teacher and fulfill the biblical roles.
strongly agree   *agree*   *not sure*   *disagree*   *strongly disagree*

Healing

I prepare my learners to meet the Lord Jesus Christ by meeting their needs as best I can.

strongly agree   agree   not sure   disagree   strongly disagree

I expect the Lord to accomplish life change in the hearts of my students.

strongly agree   agree   not sure   disagree   strongly disagree

Benediction

May the Lord Jesus Christ, who provided the way for us to believe the good news we proclaim, enable you to know and interact with truth so that you may be healthy in spirit, soul and body. Amen.

CHAPTER 2

PROCLAIM GOOD NEWS

Key Idea: Rock-solid teachers proclaim with power and impact.

When Jesus had finished saying these things, the crowds were amazed at his teaching, because he taught as one who had authority, and not as their teachers of the law.

MATTHEW 7:28-29

I don't have any influence on my class," one youth leader complained. "They don't seem to have respect for the lessons I've prepared. They don't pay attention when I speak, and nothing seems to be happening as a result of the teaching."

Why does it seem like our best efforts as teachers often result in downcast eyes, bored looks, slouching bodies, blank minds and slow obedience?

Jesus didn't seem to have this problem when He taught. At times, so many people gathered to listen to Jesus that the disciples did not have time to eat. During one particularly busy time, Jesus' family thought He'd lost His mind (see Mark 3:20-21). Jesus dealt with large crowds and even occasionally sought to get away from people by going to solitary places with His disciples (see Matt. 8:1,18).

In chapter 1, we looked briefly at Jesus' model of proclaiming, instructing and healing. As we continue exploring how to teach like Jesus, let's dig deeper into how rock-solid teachers can proclaim by following Jesus' example.

Proclaim with Authority, Attention and Amazement

Jesus taught with authority and impact. Notice how the people listening to Jesus responded. Jesus got their attention as He taught with authority, and they listened to Him in amazement.

Authority

Jesus said, "All authority in heaven and on earth has been given to me" (Matt. 28:18). While these words might be unclear to us, the people of Jesus' day certainly understood that Jesus wasn't an ordinary, tell-life-less-laws-type teacher. He had executive power!

A centurion recognized this authority in Jesus:

Lord, I do not deserve to have you come under my roof. But just say the word, and my servant will be healed. For I myself am a man under authority, with soldiers under me. I tell this one,

"Go," and he goes; and that one, "Come," and he comes. I say to my servant, "Do this," and he does it (Matt. 8:8-9).

When the Jews asked Jesus for the basis of His authority and demanded that He perform a miraculous sign to prove it, Jesus responded with a description of His resurrection: "Destroy this temple, and I will raise it again in three days" (John 2:19).

The exalted authority of Jesus can give life to our teaching and amaze our students. The problem is that we base the authority in our teaching on the following inferior foundations:

Authority based on tradition. Even in the ever-changing world of children's and youth ministry, most of us resist changing the way we've always done things. One children's worker was half serious when she declared, "Flannel graph is really the new PowerPoint!"

Adults aren't immune to a tradition-bound mind-set. Maybe you've heard the old joke, "How many adult teachers does it take to change a light bulb?" The punchline: "We just don't know—change has never happened at that level!"

Even youth workers can fall into the trap of resisting change. For example, the methods that worked a decade ago to establish small groups has become part of the *Magna Carta* of youth ministry, prohibiting any other idea except "small groups on Sunday nights at the Johnson's, Rivera's and Brown's."

Of course, tradition isn't all bad. It can do some positive things for ministry. Regular patterns of ministry can help train new workers, promote efficiency, and give a sense of security and confidence to those in ministry. But strictly adhering to tradition can stop needed initiatives, hinder enthusiasm (as if that were an ungodly trait), halt communication and create closed minds. In fact, "program paralysis"—not changing an outdated part of ministry to enhance outreach or depth—can eventually become a fatal virus.

Jesus had to deal with religious leaders who elevated the traditions of their program to the level of legalism. "Then some Pharisees and teachers of the law came to Jesus from Jerusalem and asked, 'Why do your disciples break the tradition of the elders? They don't wash their hands before they eat!' Jesus replied, 'And why do you break the command of God for the sake of your tradition?'" (Matt. 15:1).

When we base authority on outdated traditions, we become like rote scribes, causing students to needlessly struggle and preventing them from learning all they can.

Authority based on position. Do you know Sunday School teachers or youth leaders who draw an excessive sense of importance from their role? They might be struggling with an improper view of authority as related to their positions.

The same was true in Jesus' day. The scribes and Pharisees prided themselves on being teachers of the Law. Jesus recognized the authority that came with their role as teachers, but He boldly pointed out their deceptive way of life. "The teachers of the law and the Pharisees sit in Moses' seat. So you must obey them and do everything they tell you. But do not do what they do, for they do not practice what they preach" (Matt. 23:2-3).

The apostle Paul pointed out that the teachers of the Law during his era also abused their positions of authority:

> Now you, if you call yourself a Jew; if you rely on the law and brag about your relationship to God; if you know his will and approve of what is superior because you are instructed by the law; if you are convinced that you are a guide for the blind, a light for those who are in the dark, an instructor of the foolish, a teacher of infants, because you have in the law the embodiment of knowledge and truth—you, then, who teach others, do you not teach yourself? (Rom. 2:17-21).

Now, before we rush to judge the teachers of Jesus' or Paul's day, we need to look at ourselves. Many times, those of us called to be servant-leaders have mishandled our teaching role and manipulated ministry. The position of teacher is an awesome trust, and it should be used to serve our students.

Authority based on perception. The Pharisees were most concerned about how others viewed them:

As he taught, Jesus said, "Watch out for the teachers of the law. They like to walk around in flowing robes and be greeted in the marketplaces, and have the most important seats in the synagogues and the places of honor at banquets. They devour widows' houses and for a show make lengthy prayers. Such men will be punished most severely" (Mark 12:38-40).

When we fall into the trap of wanting to put ourselves on a pedestal or give ourselves more respect, we should remember Paul's words: "For we do not preach ourselves, but Jesus Christ as Lord, and ourselves as your servants for Jesus' sake" (2 Cor. 4:5). Instead of worrying about how others view us, we should be focusing on helping people see Jesus through us

Authority based on knowledge. I was once introduced as "Doctor Greg Carlson—he's paper trained!" Sometimes, people who advance in education and knowledge replace the authority they have in Jesus with what they've learned. Paul warned, "knowledge puffs up, but love builds up" (1 Cor. 8:1). Humility can be difficult for those of us who've been fortunate enough to be formally educated. So we need to be sure that our grasp of knowledge leads us to obey God and gives us a true passion for people.

The Pharisees used their learning to exclude people instead of reaching them with the knowledge of God. Because of this, Jesus warned, "Woe to you, teachers of the law and Pharisees, you hypocrites! You shut the kingdom of heaven in men's faces. You yourselves do not enter, nor will you let those enter who are trying to" (Matt. 23:13). They had become gatekeepers of relationship with the Lord instead of conduits of His grace. But by doing so, their own knowledge also prevented them from enjoying relationship with God.

Attention

Because Jesus taught with authority, people paid attention to what He said. Something authentic existed behind His words. Today, we might call it "passion." His sayings, words and doctrine were different. Even the Temple guards said, "No one ever spoke the way this man does" (John 7:46).

Whether they were simple or seasoned, the people of Jesus' day loved to hear Him speak. In his Gospel, John called Jesus the *Logos* (John 1:1). We translate this word into English as "sayings" or "words." When Jesus, the Logos, finished saying His words, people didn't have to rouse themselves from sleep. They were amazed!

The only people who seemed to struggle with giving attention to Jesus were the religious leaders of the day. I call their affliction, which still happens frequently in ministry today, the "packed dirt" principle: We become so familiar with the facts of Scripture that we neglect the power of a newly planted seed. By overlooking this power, we revert to the mechanical, resulting in teachers who proclaim life-changing truth with a frown and little joy. We seem to undergo a baptism of vinegar, causing us to never smile again. During my teen years, my pastor gave this advice to our small congregation: "If your heart is happy, notify your face!"

While the religious leaders didn't pay attention to Jesus, He had a great following among unpretentious people. He was a friend of sinners (see Luke 7:34), who excitedly followed and listened to Him. Yet those with religious backgrounds remained cautious, at best, and antagonistic to the point of plotting Jesus' death, at worst.

Jesus spoke of everyday, normal activities in His teaching. What made people pay attention to Jesus' words? Think of all the themes on which Jesus spoke. He spoke of the difference between prayers and prodigals, the Ten Commandments and taxes, the holiness of God and mercy for sinners, heavenly treasure and earthly investment, self-righteousness and sincere repentance.

Jesus moved beyond external actions to heart issues. Jesus said, "The good man brings good things out of the good stored up in his heart, and the evil man brings evil things out of the evil stored up in his heart. For out of the overflow of his heart his mouth speaks" (Luke 6:45). In other words, what we treasure in our hearts will inevitably flow out of us. This principle motivated the faithful, but the religious leaders of the day saw this internal response as a threat to the business of religion. After all, this meant that a repentant prostitute entered into the Kingdom before a self-righteous scholar.

Jesus' proclamation resulted in personal response and application. When Jesus taught, people went away with a response in their heart. Some, such as the rich young ruler, responded with sorrow (see Matt. 19:22). Others responded with great joy, such as the disciples on the Emmaus road: "Were not our hearts burning within us while he talked with us on the road and opened the Scriptures to us?" (Luke 24:32). And years later, the apostle John said that the words of Jesus were still ringing in his ears: "That which was from the beginning, which we have heard, which we have seen with our eyes, which we have looked at and our hands have touched—this we proclaim concerning the Word of life" (1 John 1:1).

Amazement

Because Jesus spoke with authority, His listeners paid attention and were amazed by His teaching. Various English translations of the Bible describe people's reactions to Jesus' teaching as "amazement," "astonishment," or "astounded." We might say that Jesus' listeners were stunned—overwhelmed with the practical application of what He proclaimed.

Jesus amazed His listeners because of the life He brought. When Jesus taught, people understood that the Great Shepherd had their interests at heart. Jesus Himself said, "I have come that they may have life, and have it to the full" (John 10:10).

That's the pattern of Jesus' teaching: authority, attention and amazement. How can we apply this to our own teaching ministry? We can take responsibility for our teaching and present our lessons with impact.

Taking Responsibility to Teach with Authority

Many children's workers find themselves mechanically going through the motions of the Sunday School lesson or children's club program. Many youth leaders feel helpless to truly address the needs of the teenagers they serve. Even many parents feel trapped by their inability to guide their children. Yet one of the most important rock-solid skills a master teacher can learn is the ability *to cause students to learn.*

We can help students learn by using our God-given authority to call for life change. When we approach learning situations, we must take responsibility for causing our students to learn.

Jesus used His authority to serve and teach His disciples. What did Jesus have authority over?

- Authority to forgive sins (see Matt. 9:6-7)
- Authority to control evil spirits (see Luke 4:36)
- Authority to judge the living and the dead (see John 5:27-29)
- Authority to command the winds and the waves (see Luke 8:22)
- Authority to give His life for the salvation of His sheep (see John 10:16-18)
- Authority to grant eternal life (see John 17:2)

Still, with all this authority, Jesus was a servant leader! He said about Himself, "For who is greater, the one who is at the table or the one who serves? Is it not the one who is at the table? But I am among you as one who serves" (Luke 22:27). Jesus used His authority to take responsibility for others!

Putting Teaching with Authority into Practice

What does teaching with authority look like? As teachers, we place our full confidence in what Scripture says as well as in the effect of that teaching. Paul told Titus, "These things speak and exhort and reprove with all authority. Let no one disregard you" (Titus 2:15, *NASB*).

Here are some practical ways we can follow the Master Teacher by taking responsibility to teach with authority as servant-leaders.

With Children

- *Offer choices of activities rather than creating a confrontation of wills.* Prepare for various responses from your students to a planned activity. This doesn't mean that you give up all control; it's more like a parent asking a child if he wants to wear a red shirt or blue shirt that day. Asking students what they'd like to do is more effective than getting a "no" answer about a single activity.

• *Determine if students respect your authority.* If your students are not open to learning, follow Jesus' example by giving them the right to choose, but highlight the consequences of their actions. If students do want to participate, the activity is a reward in itself. This will also show the positive results of learning to those who choose not to participate.

With Youth

• *"Win the right to be heard."* For years, Young Life has used this phrase in its training programs for its workers. Youth leaders shouldn't try to act like teenagers. Instead, they should seek to be caring and relationship-building adults. Some specific skills to use include:

    1. Listen well. Don't do all the talking—let the teenagers share. Let students finish their sentences, answer for themselves, get in on conversations, and be treated like real people. One youth leader always counted to five before he responded to ensure that he allowed enough time for his students to finish speaking.

    2. Build relationships by talking about the concerns, goals, interests, and experiences of the teenagers. They'll know when you sincerely care.

• *Help teenagers evaluate whether or not they're open to learning.* Sometimes, you can simply ask about their motivations. I recall one girl in a youth group I led who said she didn't realize how insensitive she'd become to her mom's instruction until we studied what it meant to take responsibility for our own actions. She said she learned that we shouldn't blame others for their harsh words or closed minds but instead examine our own hearts to see if we want to step up to obedience.

With Adults

- *Approach the learning situation with a personal sense of a call from God.* Instead of feeling like a leader recruited by others to help, assess your own sense of responsibility as a servant-leader appointed by God.

- *Ask people where they want to serve, not if they want to serve.* Instead of asking people *if* they want to be a small-group leader, ask them *where* they think God wants them to use their spiritual gifts and abilities.

With Your Own Family

- *Parenting skills start with knowing who's in charge.* When my son said no to something I wanted him to do, I said, "In a battle of the wills, God wants me to win!" He asked, "Where's that in the Bible, Dad?" My answer: "I don't know, but I'll find it!"

- *The parent is the primary educator and the first and best disciple-maker.* Take responsibility for what you believe. This applies to schooling choices, children's and youth ministry involvement, and activities around your home.

Proclaim by Presenting Your Lesson with Impact

In addition to proclaiming with authority as servant-leaders, we also become rock-solid teachers when we teach with the goal of influencing people as Jesus did.

When Jesus spoke, He was acclaimed as one of a class. "'No one ever spoke the way this man does,' the guards declared" (John 7:46). When we examine the lengthy lectures Jesus gave (for example, in Matthew 5-7; 23-25), we discover that He used lecture in a masterful way. He not only knew the Scriptures, but He also employed effective educational principles on how to use the lecture.

Take a look at some children during Sunday School or at a midweek club ministry. What are they doing? Fidgeting, acting disinterested and generally causing learning problems for others! Now ask a middle school or high school student what he or she thinks of the worship service at his or her church. What will that student say? It's *boring*!

So what's the disconnect? If Jesus used lecture effectively, why does lecture fail when teachers use it today? A quick look at Jesus' teaching principles shows how the Master Teacher succeeded.

Jesus' lectures were short. It takes 15 minutes or less to read through the Sermon on the Mount. Scholars disagree, but most believe that Jesus expected His listeners to be able to summarize what He said. What does this mean to us? As teachers, we must give students time to summarize after we finish speaking. We can accomplish this by observing how Jesus caused His disciples to learn:

- Jesus spent time with His disciples outside of His speech time. Teachers should build in techniques to review the specific points of previous learning times. When a club leader shares about verses that have been memorized during game time, this is following Jesus' example. One Sunday School teacher prompted families to recite and discuss memory verses her students were learning in class.

- Jesus often gathered His disciples for a debriefing time. "When Jesus came to the region of Caesarea Philippi, he asked his disciples, 'Who do people say the Son of Man is?'" (Matt. 16:13). One Sunday School teacher I know urges her students to share the point of the lesson with two people during the week. As a youth pastor, I often tried to gather a few core teens for a similar sharing time. We'd discuss the spiritual impact of our latest retreat on their friends and on themselves. Or we'd talk about "the good, the bad, and the ugly" of our latest youth group series of studies.

- Jesus gave His disciples reflection time. "Then, because so many people were coming and going that they did not even have a chance to eat, he said to them, 'Come with me by your-selves to a quiet place and get some rest'" (Mark 6:31). When I taught a spiritual formation class for college students, I found that a reflection journal was a good device to help them absorb what we were learning together.

Educational experts tell us that after 15 minutes, learning begins to wane for people of all ages. And after 45 minutes, learning often stops.[1] As teachers, we should resist the temptation to speak for more than about 15 minutes before introducing another method such as a story, a question, or other approach. When I have the opportunity to mentor beginning teachers, I encourage them to think of 8 to 15 minute "bursts of brilliance."

Jesus' lectures practiced sound educational techniques and devices. Most teachers don't distinguish sharply between techniques and devices. Techniques are learning activities that create variety and interest. Devices are methods and/or props that we use to do the techniques.

The principle of "chunking" is an example. Chunking is the tech-nique of taking a larger principle and dividing it into bits of information that students can master before moving on to another chunk. Jesus shared a lot of information about the Kingdom, but He used bite-size chunks to communicate it. He employed stories, illustrations, compar-isons and reflective questions as devices to help His disciples learn.

Similarly, when we help a student memorize a new Bible verse, an individual word is one chunk of information. We can connect those words to make an entire phrase into a chunk of meaning. Then, an entire verse or maybe even an entire chapter can become another chunk.

Sometimes, we also need to "un-chunk" material in order to apply a passage's teaching to specific times of obedience. We all know of stu-dents who learn Bible verses but don't seem to relate them to any life situations. By un-chunking—stringing the small bits into a larger teaching principle—we can lead students toward application of the teaching. Here are some of the tools Jesus used:

- *Parallel/contrast.* "You have heard . . . but I say" was one of Jesus' favorite devices (see Matt. 5:27-28,31-32,33-34,38-39; 26:64).

- *Repetition.* Jesus often repeated the key aspects of His teaching. I'm impressed with how often Jesus focused on the concept of faith in His teaching and learning experiences. Or consider how Jesus used repetitive climax, such as in the Beatitudes: "Blessed are the . . ." (Matt. 5:1-11).

- *Scripture reference.* Jesus often referred to Old Testament Scriptures or Old Testament concepts in His teaching, such as when He said, "You have heard that it was said, 'Do not commit adultery'" (Matt. 5:27). This also illustrates that Jesus committed vast amounts of Scripture to memory.

- *Summary.* Jesus often summarized in a masterful way: "So in everything, do to others what you would have them do to you, for this sums up the Law and the Prophets" (Matt. 7:12).

- *Thematic.* Jesus often zeroed in on one theme. Notice how many times He emphasized "the kingdom of heaven" in the Sermon on the Mount (see Matt. 5:3,10,19,20; 7:21).

- *Word pictures.* Some of Jesus' simple illustrations are still part of the vocabulary we use today. Examples include:

  - "You are the salt of the earth" (Matt. 5:13).
  - "You are the light of the world" (Matt. 5:14).
  - "A city on a hill cannot be hidden" (Matt. 5:14).
  - "Do not let your left hand know what your right hand is doing" (Matt. 6:3).

- "Store up for yourselves treasure in heaven . . . For where your treasure is, there your heart will be also" (Matt. 6:20-21).
- "Take the plank out of your own eye" (Matt. 7:5).
- "False prophets . . . come to you in sheep's clothing, but inwardly they are ferocious wolves" (Matt. 7:15).
- "By their fruit you will recognize them" (Matt. 7:20).
- "Neither do men pour new wine into old wineskins" (Matt. 9:17).
- "Be as shrewd as snakes and as innocent as doves" (Matt. 10:16).
- "Take my yoke upon you and learn from me" (Matt. 11:29).
- "It is easier for a camel to go through the eye of a needle than for a rich man to enter the kingdom of God" (Matt. 19:24).

Jesus' lectures were interspersed with other methods. Jesus' talks rarely stood alone. He used other means—what we might call learning activities or creative methods—to communicate His teachings. Some of the other methods Jesus used were:

- *Discussion/debate.* Jesus' disciples often debated—heatedly—the truths that Jesus taught. "They began to discuss this among themselves, saying, 'He said that because we did not bring any bread.' But Jesus, aware of this, said, 'You men of little faith, why do you discuss among yourselves that you have no bread?'" (Matt. 16:7-8, *NASB*).

- *Music.* We don't know if Jesus used this method often, but He closed His upper-room discourse with a hymn.

- *Questions and answers.* Jesus was often open to questions from the people He was teaching. The well-known story of the Good Samaritan was prompted by a lawyer who asked, "And who is my neighbor?" (Luke 10:29). In another instance, after Jesus described the coming Kingdom, the disciples wanted to know when it would happen (see Matt. 24:3).

- *Stories.* Jesus' parables pack such power that people still tell the stories Jesus told. (We'll explore the power of storytelling in chapter 3.)

- *Visuals/object lessons.* Jesus often used everyday items or people to emphasize His point. "See how the lilies of the field grow" (Matt. 6:28). "He took a little child and had him stand among them" (Mark. 9:36). "They brought the coin, and he asked them, 'Whose portrait is this?'" (Mark 12:16).

Putting Jesus' Method of Lecture into Practice

Here are some practical ways you can imitate Jesus, the Master Teacher, by improving the ways you lecture when you teach.

With Children

- *Keep it short.* Keep your lecture to a minute for each year of age, capping at about 15 minutes. This will help you keep your students' attention and will focus your own teaching.

- *Encourage children to help with the visual aids of a lecture.* One children's pastor has fifth graders take turn advancing PowerPoint slides. Kids also love to have a hand in preparing a room for the talk or story.

With Youth

- *Form listening teams.* Have certain teenagers in the group listen for specific items during a lecture. This heightens the students' motivation and also highlights the important aspects of your lesson.

- *Use music in your lecture.* One guest speaker formed the outline of his message from a contemporary Christian song.

With Adults

- *Lace your lecture with other methods.* Incorporate a discussion time, a question and answer time, and even visual and object lessons. Remember the old adage: "There's no such thing as a bad method, except the one you use all the time!" In other words, mix things up.

- *Allow for response time.* We often underestimate the power of quiet reflection after a lecture. Encourage people to journal about the lesson, or urge people to spend time in silent prayer as they review their notes.

With Your Own Family

- *Get feedback.* Parents are famous for lecturing their kids. Try asking, "What did you hear me say just now?" This provides a feedback loop and measures instruction from parent to child.

- *Encourage children to take notes of key points.* I know a parent who had her children take notes on a speech the president gave. Then, they had a conversation about the main points that each child recorded.

Self-Check

Before you turn to chapter 3, take a few minutes to evaluate how you're fulfilling your role as a rock-solid teacher in the area of proclamation. Just between you and God, rate how you're doing at proclaiming with authority and impact. Spend some time in prayer asking God to help you grow in areas in which you're struggling.

Proclaiming with Authority

If my students aren't learning, I try to change circumstances and my style so that I can gain their attention and encourage a response.

strongly agree   agree   not sure   disagree   strongly disagree

I sense a calling from God to teach truth in my class or group. As a teacher, I assume the care and feeding of my students.

strongly agree   agree   not sure   disagree   strongly disagree

I expect each student to respond to what God is teaching him or her.

strongly agree   agree   not sure   disagree   strongly disagree

Proclaiming by Presenting Your Lesson with Impact

I prepare lessons with an awareness of the strengths of my presentation (and the weaknesses) so I can proclaim truth with clarity and conviction.

strongly agree   agree   not sure   disagree   strongly disagree

I use other methods in my lecture to ensure strong learning.

strongly agree   agree   not sure   disagree   strongly disagree

Benediction

May the One who has all authority in heaven and on Earth give you power to influence the lives of your students. May you find great joy in the skills of teaching that you have, and grow to have increasing life change occur in those you teach by the power of the Master Teacher. Amen.

CHAPTER 3

TEACH TO LEARN

*Key Idea: Rock-solid teachers instruct
students toward obedience.*

*Then Jesus came to them and said, "All authority in heaven and on earth
has been given to me. Therefore go and make disciples of all nations,
baptizing them in the name of the Father and of the Son and of the Holy
Spirit, and teaching them to obey everything I have commanded you.
And surely I am with you always, to the very end of the age."*

MATTHEW 28:18-20

Awise and effective fourth-grade Sunday School teacher worked with his eager students as they memorized Ephesians 4:32: "Be kind and compassionate to one another, forgiving each other, just as in Christ God forgave you."

In the middle of reciting the verse, the teacher stopped his students and asked, "What do you think this verse means? How would you use this verse to obey God at school this week?" A lively discussion followed that focused on what it means to stay tenderhearted or compassionate in a "I couldn't care less" world at school. One student asked what it meant to forgive as God forgave.

This teacher taught like the Master!

As teachers, we have a huge responsibility to help our students understand what it means to obey God. Although it involves the addition of just a few words, there's a huge difference between "teaching them to obey everything I have commanded" (Jesus' words and the focus of this chapter) and "teaching them everything" (what too many of us try).

How did Jesus teach so that people responded by obeying His commands? Let's look at Jesus' teaching ministry and several methods He used to create an "obey what you know" learning situation.

Using Parables to Instruct Toward Obedience

Parables are the storytelling method of choice of our Lord. A parable could be defined as a brief story that will stand alone, like a self-contained module that appeals to the thinking and attitudes of the hearers. There are other ways to tell stories, of course, but we will focus on the parable telling (or storytelling) of Jesus. I see them as one and the same. Parables are a particular kind of story.

When the disciples asked Jesus why He told stories, He answered, "I tell these stories, because people see what I do, but they don't really see. They hear what I say, but they don't really hear, and they don't understand" (Matt. 13:13, *NLT*). In other words, Jesus told stories to prompt listeners to obey.

As teachers, we need to make sure that we help students make the connection between storytelling and obeying God. All too often, we tell stories but don't encourage students to practice what God says.

Jesus used parables for several reasons:

Jesus used parables to distinguish the teachable from the unteachable. Jesus used stories to train His followers, but the same stories often confounded His enemies. When people were unwilling to learn, a parable demonstrated that they were indeed resisting. Jesus even stated that if someone didn't keep or obey His words, it was the same as losing them: "Consider carefully how you listen. Whoever has will be given more; whoever does not have, even what he thinks he has will be taken from him" (Luke 8:18).

I once attended a New Testament seminar offered by Walk Thru the Bible Ministries. As the instructor spoke, he placed his hand over one eye to indicate "Parables Start." Those who wish to see, see more clearly; while those who are resistant, are blinded more.

Jesus used parables to provide a memorable way to continue obedient learning. The disciples demonstrated a growing confidence in what they learned and applied. After Jesus explained the parable of the sower to His disciples, He urged them to listen and carefully apply what they'd heard (see Luke 8:18). Apparently they remembered, because decades later, the apostle Peter still referred to God's Word as an imperishable seed (see 1 Pet. 1:23).

Stories have tremendous power! Most of us remember a story our pastor or small-group leader shared more than we recall the point of the sermon or Bible study. When we tell stories in our teaching, we need to recognize the work God is doing in our students' lives. We also need to celebrate the Holy Spirit's work before we move on to new things.

Jesus used parables to cultivate a readiness to learn. Although the Pharisees proved to be unwilling hearers, the disciples were eager learners. Jesus' parables created the heart attitude that the disciples needed to learn about the way of Christ. Mark 4 outlines a series of parables, ending with this summary:

> With many similar parables Jesus spoke the word to them, as much as they could understand. He did not say anything to them without using a parable. But when he was alone with his own disciples, he explained everything (vv. 33-34).

I'm often invited to speak to youth groups. At one particular event, the coordinator told me, "I want you to know that these kids won't listen to any Bible teaching." So I started by telling several stories of kids in my first youth group, related the tale of my arm accident during my high school days, and ended with the story of Jesus and the rich young ruler (see Matt. 19:16-25). While some in the group continued to be disinterested and even rude, others responded. The stories led to a lively discussion of how teenagers can serve Christ during high school and of the importance of sharing the gospel with friends.

The Structure of Parables

There are many ways to tell stories, and we can certainly be creative. But I believe we can greatly improve the stories we tell by following Jesus' examples. When we dissect the way that Jesus told parables, we can see several profound principles about how to tell our own stories:

The source of Jesus' illustrations were often imagination. Jesus rarely used personal examples, and while He regularly used material from Scripture, He only occasionally used historical examples. That's the opposite of what many storytellers do today.

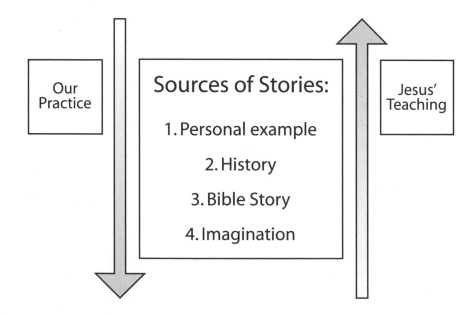

The opening (first 10 seconds) of Jesus' stories established the setting. Too many times when we tell stories, we don't answer any of the six journalistic questions: Who? What? When? Where? Why? How? Take Jesus' well-known parable about the sower and the seed. In 10 seconds, you can read about this much:

> A sower went out to sow his seed: and as he sowed, some fell by the way side; and it was trodden down, and the fowls of the air devoured it. And some fell upon a rock (Luke 8:5-6).

Now ask the six questions. At least half are answered in these few words:

1. *Who?* The sower.
2. *What?* Went out to sow.
3. *When?* Not answered, but probably at sowing time.
4. *Where?* His field.
5. *Why?* Not answered. Jesus will use this to illustrate spiritual receptivity.
6. *How?* Jesus develops the details to fit His teaching purposes.

The opening of Jesus' stories also directed the listener's interest. By establishing the basic plot in the first few seconds, Jesus could then tell a longer story. However, none of Jesus' recorded stories would take more than three minutes to tell, while the shortest would take just 20 seconds. As teachers, if we want students to remember what we've taught, we need to be thinking "quick."

The final sentences of Jesus' parables prompted a response from listeners. Note some of His methodology:

- He usually didn't have to state the main point, because it was obvious from the story.

- He usually established the analogy in the first sentence. For example, "The kingdom of heaven is like . . ." (Matt. 13:31).

• He often ended His stories with a convincing question: "How is he then his son?" (Luke 20:44, *KJV*).

Putting Jesus' Method of Telling Stories into Practice

As we look at how to use Jesus' storytelling methods in our own teaching, I like the way Eugene Peterson translates Jesus' answer of why He told stories:

> You've been given insight into God's kingdom. You know how it works. Not everybody has this gift, this insight; it hasn't been given to them. Whenever someone has a ready heart for this, the insights and understandings flow freely. But if there is no readiness, any trace of receptivity soon disappears. That's why I tell stories: to create readiness, to nudge the people toward receptive insight (Matt. 13:11-13, *THE MESSAGE*).

As rock-solid teachers, we can use the following methods to nudge our students toward "receptive insight."

With Children

• *Listen to other storytellers.* Try imitating their methods to improve your own style.

• *Ask children to share a Bible story they heard in church or in another class.* Their interpretation will prompt good discussion.

• *Capitalize on educational research that shows children as young as three have "scripts" they organize their learning around.*[1] This means that storytelling is an exceptionally strong learning mode for children. Learn to tell stories and involve children in them.

• *Use the following guidelines for telling stories to children:*

▫ Know the material.

▫ Don't memorize; just tell the story in your own words.

▫ Practice, practice, practice . . .

▫ Involve children in storytelling by acting it out, using sound effects, using the Bible and researching the stories together.[2]

With Youth

• *Let teenagers tell the story.* You can use several different techniques to accomplish this:

▫ Start a story and have others finish it. Gather your students in small groups of four to eight individuals. Start a story, and then let another continue it until each person has had a turn. The first person can veto the direction of the story, but only one time.

▫ Ask teenagers to tell the Bible story you're using in your lesson. You won't be teaching something they already know, and their involvement will increase what they'll learn.

▫ Assign a team of reporters to "interview" a Bible character and act out their work for the rest of the class.

• *Adapt Youth for Christ USA's training for evangelism called "three story evangelism."* In essence, this training encourages students to listen to another person's story, tell their own story, and then tell the story of Jesus. Too often, we tell the story of Christ or our own story, but we don't really listen to the person we're seeking to serve.

With Adults

• *Practice telling stories.* Take turns telling about 15 seconds of a personal story. Then have the storyteller answer at least three of the six journalistic questions from those 15 seconds:

1. Who?

2. What?

3. When?

4. Where?

5. Why?

6. How?

This is a great way to sharpen illustrations in stories, because a focused beginning generates a clear model for setting the context. You can also encourage adult students to share the ending or moral to their story. It can be profound or silly, but it's likely to be memorable.

- *Go deeper with personal stories.* My wife, Donna, has small-group members draw timelines of their lives. As each person tells their life story—complete with highs and lows—the group members get to know and understand each other. Both laughter and tears abound. This technique not only helps group members get acquainted, but it also teaches deep lessons of spiritual growth, struggle, failure and success.

With Your Own Family

- *Tell "family stories."* This is a great way to pass down the values of your family. Encourage members of the older generations to start telling about "the way it was." You might want to videotape grandparents and other senior relatives talking about their early church experiences, their courtship and establishment of a family, and their fresh life in Christ and how it has been sustained. These priceless moments will be treasured by each generation. Psalm 78:2-7 provides a nice description of how important this is:

> I will open my mouth in parables, I will utter hidden things, things from of old—what we have heard and known, what our fathers have told us. We will not hide them from their children; we will tell the next generation the praiseworthy deeds of the LORD, his power, and the wonders he has done. He decreed statutes for Jacob and established the law in Israel, which he commanded our forefathers to teach their children, so the next generation would know them, even the children yet to be born, and they in turn would tell their children. Then they would put their trust in God and would not forget his deeds but would keep his commands.

- *Create your family's record of stories.* Have each member tell an important story about the family. Mom or Dad can begin and then allow all members to have their chance. Don't be afraid to tell a story more than once. Sometimes the best stories are worth repeating again and again.

Using Questions to Instruct Toward Obedience

Jesus was a master storyteller and also a master question-asker! When we ask questions, we usually want a verbal or written response. But sometimes questions inspire internal reflection. Questions also provide an automatic feedback loop in communication. They give teachers a chance to understand their students and provide a way to offer further insights that lead to obedience.

Perhaps no more powerful tool than questions exist for challenging our thinking, helping us place attitudes in proper priority, and prompting us to obey. Consider some of the ways that Jesus taught with questions:

Jesus used questions to clarify and deepen thinking. Even as a child, Jesus asked questions that clarified priorities: "Did you not know that I must be about My Father's business?" (Luke 2:49, *NKJV*). As a young learner, Jesus was found in the Temple "sitting among the teachers, listening to them and asking them questions" (Luke 2:46).

I remember asking my father and grandfather questions that came up in my own personal Bible study. The lively discussions were highlights of my younger years. I didn't know how unique my heritage was until many years later.

During Jesus' most intense leadership-development times with the disciples, He used rhetorical questions: "What good is it for a man to gain the whole world, and yet lose or forfeit his very self?" (Luke 9:25). He didn't expect the disciples to answer; He was trying to jumpstart their thinking.

Even when He was on trial, Jesus sought to teach by clarifying and deepening His judge's opinion: "'Is that your own idea,' Jesus asked, 'or did others talk to you about me?'" (John 18:34). Jesus used questions to clarify priorities, get others to think and evaluate information, all for the overarching purpose of increasing people's knowledge of God.

Jesus used questions to reveal and prompt a proper attitude. Professor Howard Hendricks was once conducting a seminar for a group of pastors and spouses and asked, "What's the single most important lesson Jesus sought to teach?" The answer: "Faith."

Faith was a constant emphasis of Jesus' teaching. Jesus was looking for these qualities in the attitudes of those who answered His questions:

- *Motives.* When teaching about the golden rule, Jesus asked, "If you love those who love you, what credit is that to you? Even 'sinners' love those who love them. And if you do good to those who are good to you, what credit is that to you? Even 'sinners' do that. And if you lend to those from whom you expect repayment, what credit is that to you? Even 'sinners' lend to 'sinners,' expecting to be repaid in full" (Luke 6:32-34).

- *The condition of the learner's heart.* When revealing the hypocrisy of the Pharisees, Jesus said, "You foolish people! Did not the one who made the outside make the inside also?" (Luke 11:40).

Jesus used questions to guide actions toward the proper outcome. The "proper outcome" was that Jesus wanted people to obey His commands. He wanted them to act with conviction. For example:

- After Jesus told a short parable, He used questions to help Simon realize the error of his ways (see Luke 7:42-47).

- After Jesus calmed the storm, He turned to His fearful disciples and asked, "Where is your faith?" (Luke 8:25).

- In the conclusion to the parable of the Good Samaritan, Jesus asked, "Which of these three do you think was a neighbor to the man who fell into the hands of robbers?" (Luke 10:36).

- When the synagogue ruler criticized Jesus for healing on the Sabbath, the Lord answered him, "You hypocrites! Doesn't each of you on the Sabbath untie his ox or donkey from the stall and lead it out to give it water? Then should not this woman, a daughter of Abraham, whom Satan has kept bound for eighteen long years, be set free on the Sabbath day from what bound her?" (Luke 13:15-16).

- Jesus also used this kind of questioning to prompt students to explain the correct action. When the Pharisees pointed out that the disciples of other teachers fasted and prayed while Jesus' disciples did not, Jesus answered, "Can you make the guests of the bridegroom fast while he is with them?" (Luke 5:34). And in his lesson about the wise and foolish builders, Jesus asked, "Why do you call me, 'Lord, Lord,' and do not do what I say?" (Luke 6:46).

Jesus used questions to establish Scripture as the reference point. Jesus urged His students to look to Scripture's teaching for decision making, thinking, attitude development and guidelines for action. This was the most profound use of questions in Jesus' teaching! There are numerous instances where He brought the learner back to the Scriptures with a question.

Perhaps one of Jesus' favorite questions regarding Scripture was "have you not read?" He used it when confronting the Pharisees about working on the Sabbath by eating in the grain fields (see Luke 6:3). He used it when instructing the young lawyer, "On one occasion an expert in the law stood up to test Jesus. 'Teacher,' he asked, 'what must I do to inherit eternal life?' 'What is written in the Law?' he replied. 'How do you read it?'" (Luke 10:25-26). And Jesus answered the Herodians and Pharisees with the same question in relation to the resurrection (see Matt. 21:42).

When Jesus employed questions in His teaching, He followed these effective practices:

- He rarely asked knowledge questions (such as who, where and when) but often asked probing questions (such as why and how). Probing questions "promote a deeper understanding of content, delving . . . less on the subject and more on individual students."[3]

- He rarely used "yes" and "no" questions.

- He used pauses effectively. In other words, He waited longer than we typically do before continuing. Most teachers wait just nine-tenths of a second until they begin another verbal statement or question. By changing this habit to a three-second wait, you'll see a significant change in how your students answer your questions.[4]

- He asked versatile questions. Sometimes He began His teaching with a question, sometimes He ended His lesson with a question, and sometimes He reinforced His main points with questions.

- He urged His followers to ask questions of Him, encouraged them to ask questions of each other, and asked questions of them.

Putting Jesus' Method of Using Questions into Practice

As rock-solid teachers, we can use questions to get simple responses. But we can also ask questions to prompt students to reflect, to get feedback, to understand a challenge our students face, and to lead our students toward obedience. Here are some specific ideas.

With Children

- *Use a question box.* Set up a question box to encourage students to ask questions about a lesson, issues they're facing at home or school, or any other questions they want to ask.

- *Urge children to answer questions in a group.* You might send small groups of students on treasure hunts to search for answers to clues or questions that you've prepared.

With Youth

- *Invite the senior pastor.* Ask the senior pastor of your church to attend youth-group meetings and allow the teenagers to ask him "anything."

- *Prompt the discussion.* Teenagers love to study the Bible once they know the right questions to ask as they study. I've used the "Class Discussion" suggestions from Henrietta C. Mears's *What the Bible Is All About* with good success. The founder of Gospel Light shares how prompting the discussion of students is an effective way to learn:

  □ Hand out discussion topics for the following week.
  □ Discern when an issue raised by the class is vital to their faith instead of a mere oddity to quibble over.
  □ Ask the students to turn in the questions they'd like answers to, and then guide the discussion.[5]

Another great resource is Wes Haystead's *Bible 101*.[6] This book employs the use of questions to aid students in studying the Bible for themselves.

With Adults

• *Eliminate the lecture.* Teach a whole class using only questions.

• *Ask, "What have you learned?"* You can follow this by encouraging students to take something home from the class. This helps adult students learn to process their own learning.

With Your Own Family

• *Observe how educational programs use questions to teach.* Programs such as *Sesame Street, Blue's Clues* and *VeggieTales* often employ questions. Usually, these questions have been researched for effectiveness with children. Imitate the appropriate use of questions with your own children.

• *Ask questions during a special family night or at mealtimes.* On the way home from work, I would enjoy thinking up "Dad's famous question" to ask my children when I got home. It prompted each of us to share about what was going on in our lives. Some sample questions:

  ▫ Who's the most important person you met this last week? Why?
  ▫ If you could go anywhere on vacation, where would you go?
  ▫ What do you enjoy about our church?
  ▫ What TV program (or movie or DVD) taught you something recently that reinforced what you've learned in youth group?
  ▫ What do you think you would like to be doing in five years? In 10 years? In 20 years?

- What's one thing you appreciate about each member of our family?
- What's your favorite place on Earth?
- What's something you learned today at school?
- If you could interview anyone in history (from the Bible, from history, or someone alive today) who would it be, and what would you ask that person?
- What's your favorite snack? Meal? Breakfast?
- What room in our house would you change if you could?
- Who in our extended family gives sincere compliments?
- How has a verse you've studied in Sunday School or youth group been helpful to you?

Self-Check

Before you turn to chapter 4, take a few minutes to evaluate how you're fulfilling your role as a rock-solid teacher in the area of instructing students toward obedience. Just between you and God, rate how you're doing at instructing using storytelling and questions. Spend some time in prayer asking God to help you grow in areas in which you're struggling.

Instructing with Storytelling

With the teaching I do in my class or group, I see students learning to obey.

strongly agree   *agree*   *not sure*   *disagree*   *strongly disagree*

I use stories that lead students to seek God's will and not just to entertain.

strongly agree   *agree*   *not sure*   *disagree*   *strongly disagree*

I tell stories to capture the interest of my students by using variety and speaking with skill and passion.

strongly agree   *agree*   *not sure*   *disagree*   *strongly disagree*

Instructing with Questions

I ask questions that stimulate thinking, evaluation and life change in my students.

strongly agree   *agree*   *not sure*   *disagree*   *strongly disagree*

I use questions to get students involved in what I'm teaching.

strongly agree   agree   not sure   disagree   strongly disagree

Benediction

May the Master Storyteller enable you to tell your stories in such a way that questions of learning will be prompted, and may you confidently be ready to answer anyone who asks a reason for the hope in you, until He comes. Amen.

CHAPTER 4

BRING HEALING

Key Idea: Rock-solid teachers bring healing as Jesus did—through gracious words and healthy relationships.

All spoke well of him and were amazed at the gracious words that came from his lips. "Isn't this Joseph's son?" they asked. Jesus said to them, "Surely you will quote this proverb to me: 'Physician, heal yourself! Do here in your hometown what we have heard that you did in Capernaum.'"

LUKE 4:22-23

I identified with Dean, a friend from my college days who had physical disabilities. As I mentioned, when I was 16, I had a farm accident that damaged my arm. So I had some empathy for Dean and his physical limitations.

Dean entered college on probation. Not only did the school wonder if Dean could cut it, but Dean also wondered that himself. He didn't have a lot of confidence. Some of the physical limitations were rather distracting at first and few people wanted to take the time to help Dean. In the first Bible class he took, he didn't show much promise. He seemed destined to flunk out.

But Dean knew about the healing power of God in his life. And he knew how to persevere! God prepared him through some focused attention from a professor, encouragement from a few fellow students, and tutoring from another professor's daughter—whom Dean eventually married.

It seemed that God provided healing for Dean as he learned. Dean pieced together enough credits to earn an associate's degree and headed off to serve as a youth pastor. He loved the teenagers in his group, and because of his own limitations, he related to some kids who never would have been reached by the typical "All-American" youth leader.

Eventually, Dean and his wife started raising a family. Although, as far as I know, the Lord never saw fit to remove Dean's physical disabilities, he continues to serve as a youth worker. That's the amazing healing power of the Lord.

The Healing Ministry of Jesus

In chapter 1, we defined the healing ministry of Jesus in two dimensions: the caretaker and the curer. As a review, we said that the *caretaker* dimension of Jesus' ministry has the following three components:

1. *Jesus served in His healing.* He cared for others' needs and met their needs to prepare them to learn.

2. *Jesus deepened perspectives in His teaching.* He used physical healing to help the disciples expand their viewpoint of people.

Jesus met needs to prime people for truth.

3. *Jesus lifted through His healing.* He met needs in order to place people before the Lord.

The *curative* aspect of Jesus' ministry also has three aspects:

1. *The spiritual healing of people.* Jesus taught that the spiritual dimension of life is so important that it doesn't compare with physical health. We must seek to be spiritual healers in our teaching ministry.

2. *The inner healing (wholeness) of people.* God provides an inner holiness or wholeness through His sanctifying work.

3. *The physical healing of people.* God uses physical ailments and restoration of health to bring awareness and receptivity to His work.

Let's dig a little deeper into the ways rock-solid teachers can bring healing. We can follow the example of Jesus—the Master Teacher—and offer healing through the gracious words we speak and through the healthy relationships we build.

Gracious Words for Healing

Like a soothing ointment, when Jesus spoke gracious words, those who received the words experienced healing! Can you imagine the joy and strength that Mary experienced when Jesus spoke her name in front of the Garden tomb? Previously, Jesus had healed Mary spiritually, casting out seven demons (see Mark 16:9).

Or what about the power and health flowing to the woman at the well because of Jesus' gracious words? Do you hear the joy in Jesus' compliment of the centurion's faith as his servant was healed with a word: "I tell you, I have not found such great faith even in Israel" (Luke 7:9-10)?

Although Jesus' words gave joy to the hearers, He faced some trouble. His hometown crowd didn't know how to deal with their local son. They wanted to put the Lord Jesus Christ into a safe, normal relationship grid. They could understand Jesus as "Joseph's son," but not what His healing miracles were pointing to: Jesus as the promised Messiah! Someone greater than Abraham (the founder of their faith structure) was among them. As a result, "The people in the synagogue were furious. . . . They got up, drove him out of the town, and took him to the brow of the hill on which the town was built, in order to throw him down the cliff" (Luke 4:28-29).

Most of us feel similar discomfort when we think of Jesus' healing ministry. We hesitate to speak of Christ's healing work in our teaching. But we shouldn't feel uncomfortable at all, because spiritual healing—the forgiveness of sins that brings people into a right relationship with God—happens through the blood of Christ. Inner healing comes as this same grace takes root in a believer. The apostle Paul described how we live out this inner reality: "So then, just as you received Christ Jesus as Lord, continue to live in him, rooted and built up in him, strengthened in the faith as you were taught, and overflowing with thankfulness" (Col. 2:6-7).

Healthy Relationships for Healing

Our caretaker role as rock-solid teachers involves preparing, deepening and lifting our students, just as Jesus did in His ministry. In addition to speaking gracious words, we must also build healthy relationships with our learners. Healthy relationships provide healing in the following ways:

Healthy relationships heal resistance. Sometimes, a hard or unfeeling response indicates a learner's resistant and disrespectful attitude. This was certainly the case with the Pharisees' and Sadducees' attitude toward Jesus (see Matt. 16:1-4).

What do we do when a student tests us? I remember how upset I got when two of the key leaders in our youth group invited the students over to their house to watch horror movies. Unfortunately, I was on a trip for our church that weekend and didn't hear about it until I returned—and did I ever hear about it from some of the parents!

I got together with the two guys and discovered that they were "bored with the whole youth group scene." It prompted some good changes in the way we ran the ministry. We began focusing on more teaching about Christ, serving Him, and challenging those who'd known Christ a long time to step up and be leaders. The caretaker ministry response involved taking responsibility to cause these resistant students to experience a more authentic walk with Jesus.

Healthy relationships heal doubts. Skepticism and doubt can lead to good learning when students test the waters regarding matters of faith. Think of those who came to hear John the Baptist (see Luke 7:24-35), or the case of the lawyer who Jesus questioned with the story of the Good Samaritan (see Luke 10:25-37). When people were set against Jesus, He told stories. To those who were investigating, He told the truth about Himself. To those who were doubtful, He asked questions and raised challenges. And Jesus provided evidence of God's work!

What do we do with students who test us because of their doubt? My sixth-grade son once expressed some questions during our evening prayer-before-bedtime: "What if all this stuff about Jesus is made up?" I explained that Jesus' being raised from the dead proves that He's God, and therefore we can trust His words. "Oh," is all my son said as he rolled over and went to sleep. Meet doubts with evidence and experience.

Healthy relationships heal confusion. Jesus continued to teach the disciples even when they missed the point. He repeated His major teaching of the cross and the resurrection even though they didn't get it (see Matt. 16:21; 17:23; 20:17-19). And He stabilized those who failed—like Peter—when they didn't even trust themselves (see John 21).

How do we teach students who are confused? A woman in an adult Sunday School class experienced major levels of stress and confusion during a nasty divorce proceeding. Her husband had been unfaithful and then had blamed her for the problem. When she chatted with her teacher and his wife over coffee, it became clear that her bitterness was hindering her growth in Christ. Through a lot of Scripture reading, prayer and counseling, forgiveness finally took root. She was able to receive healing from this roadblock in her relationship with the Lord, and she now cares for and disciples other women who are struggling with the same issues. Meet confusion with patience and persistence.

Healthy relationships heal motives. Some people who followed Jesus were just looking for a free lunch (see John 6:26). Others sought to meet Jesus because of a need for healing, such as the woman who touched Jesus' cloak (see Luke 8:43-48) or the centurion who had a sick servant (Luke 7:1-10). Still others came to Jesus in the grip of grief, like Jairus's daughter (see Luke 8:41-56) or Lazarus's family (see John 11:1-3).

What do we do with those who seem to be seeking help superficially? I remember a guy in college who came to our youth group when one of the young women in our core leadership team invited him. I wasn't sure if he attended because he had sincere spiritual interest or if he just wanted to get to know her better! In any case, he kept coming, and eventually his motivation changed. And he changed as he came to know the Lord and grew in Christ. Meet people with shallow needs by continuing to teach and deepen them until they meet Christ.

Healthy relationships heal convictions. When John the Baptist told two of his disciples that Jesus was the Lamb of God, the disciples followed Christ and asked to know where He was staying (see John 1:35-38). In our day, this would be like saying, "Can we hang out with you?" At other times, Jesus invited learners to follow Him (see Matt. 4:19). The idea of being a "disciple" involves being a believer, a pupil, an imitator and a person who sacrifices to follow (see Matt. 11:29-30; Luke 6:40; 14:27; John 6:69).

How should we encourage those who faithfully follow? When I served as a pastor, I remember a time when I was so busy counseling people in troubled marriages and visiting people who were sick that I had little time to develop the leaders of the church. I finally realized that by mentoring and discipling these willing leaders, I would actually be less swamped in the long term. I could equip these leaders to do the ministry I was struggling to accomplish and that they were ready and willing to take on. Followers of Christ deserve our attention and affection. It brings healing and purpose to their lives.

Healthy relationships heal confidence. Jesus appointed the disciples with this job description: "And he ordained twelve, that they should be with him, and that he might send them forth to preach, and to have power to heal sicknesses, and to cast out devils" (Mark 3:14-15, *KJV*). Not only were these chosen followers to be with Jesus to learn and prepare for ministry, but also He wanted to send them out to multiply ministry for the Lord.

How should we instill confidence in those who feel called to ministry? Sometimes, it just takes good observation skills. An international student at the college where I taught showed great promise. He learned English to the point that he sounded like a native English-speaker—minus the slang. He was quite articulate in face-to-face meetings, but he struggled in the classroom. One day, I noticed him squinting when I wrote an assignment on the whiteboard. A trip with the dean of students to the eye doctor and a pair of glasses resulted in learning that matched this student's potential!

Putting Jesus' Model of Healing into Practice

Here are some practical ideas for bringing healing into the lives of your students:

With Children

- *Kneel down to look children in the eye.* Get down to their level if possible. Too often, we try to build relationships with children from the stratosphere—at least that's what it looks like to them!

- *Build healing and healthy relationships into teaching.* Use children's ministry speaker and trainer Ivy Beckwith's five characteristics of a child's sense of community to build healing and healthy relationships in your teaching ministry:

  1. Belonging: "A sense of belonging is of paramount importance to children. Children need to know that when they walk through the door of their church

building, they are welcome and valued as much as the
adults."

2. Trust: "While children may not understand the type
   of leadership or governance a faith community has,
   they will understand if the community is a safe and
   secure place for them."

3. Sharing gifts: "Too often we think of children's ministry as doing something for our children. We need to
   expand our thinking to see that it is also working
   with our children and allowing them to minister to
   the adults."

4. Citizenship: "We need to be intentional about helping
   [children] respect people who are different from them
   and helping them understand that part of being a
   faithful person is being concerned about the larger,
   extended community and the world."

5. Story: "Children are not born knowing any of these
   stories or knowing they have a story to create. Stories
   are communicated to them by the older generations
   of the community, and the stories must be communicated to children in meaningful ways."[1]

With Youth

• *Remember the names of the students in your ministry.* As someone
who has to work at this, I've found these suggestions from
youth-worker trainer Doug Fields to be helpful:

  □ Say the name quickly.
  □ Use the name frequently in conversation.
  □ Ask a question using the name: "Jana, how did you
    hear about tonight?"
  □ Say the name again when you close the conversation.
  □ Relate the name to someone you knew previously or to
    a place.

□ Take pictures of the person, write his or her names on the back of the pictures, and use them as flash cards.

□ Look closely and attentively at the person as he or she speaks and try to find distinct features about him or her.

□ Do something fun with the person—you always remember someone more when you're laughing and having fun!

□ When all else fails, give the person a nickname that is appropriate or sounds like his or her name (such as Hector = Nectar).

□ Ask for identifying information about the person.

□ Study the student's face while you're being introduced.

□ Ask God to help you remember and care (we remember what's important to us).

□ Write down the name on your hand, on a card, or on scrap paper—the act of writing will help you retain it.

□ Ask students to test you on it.[2]

• *Set aside discussion time.* Set aside 10 to 15 minutes before and after your youth group's meeting to talk with the students. Have specific questions ready and stay involved with a small group of students.

With Adults

• *Make a record of your encouraging words, when possible.* "Write your positive words, speak your negative." I don't know how many times that advice from my pastor during seminary days has guided my ministry. You want a record of positive words, *not* a permanent record of faults.

• *Be careful when you teach using humor.* Whoever said "sticks and stones can break my bones, but words will never hurt me" was a liar! Words said in humor can cause great harm. I often find my wit ahead of my wisdom. Learning to use gracious speech and avoid coarse jesting has helped my teaching ministry.

With Your Own Family

- *Develop relationships at home.* Spend time at home developing relationships using these suggestions from the workbook *Shepherding Parents:*

  - Start your evening with prayer.
  - Play games or do an activity together.
  - Eat together.
  - Have a Bible lesson as a family.
  - Close in prayer.[3]

- *Be prepared to lead your children to Christ.* Children's workers at your church can equip you to do this, or log on to www.awana.org for information on how to make this clear. Another fine resource is Larry Fowler's (Executive Director of Program and Training at Awana Clubs International) book *Rock-Solid Kids*, especially chapters 7 and 8.[4]

Self-Check

Before you turn to chapter 5, take a few minutes to evaluate how you're fulfilling your role as a rock-solid teacher in the area of bringing God's healing through your teaching. Just between you and God, rate how you're doing at speaking gracious words and building healthy relationships. Spend some time in prayer asking God to help you grow in areas in which you're struggling.

Speaking Gracious Words

I try to remember students' names while I'm teaching.

strongly agree　　　*agree*　　　*not sure*　　　*disagree*　　　*strongly disagree*

I look for inner qualities of character and don't make judgments based on external appearance.

strongly agree   agree   not sure   disagree   strongly disagree

I encourage others with positive statements and don't just point out areas where they need to improve.

strongly agree   agree   not sure   disagree   strongly disagree

Building Healthy Relationships

I take seriously the responsibility to build relationships with my students so that I can respond to their resistance, doubts or confusion.

strongly agree   agree   not sure   disagree   strongly disagree

I believe that it's just as important to prepare myself relationally as I do intellectually—developing a proper relationship with God, other believers and those in the world.

strongly agree   agree   not sure   disagree   strongly disagree

I find myself forgiving others even when they haven't asked for it because I know that bitterness can cause healing to evaporate.

strongly agree   agree   not sure   disagree   strongly disagree

Benediction

May the Great Physician give you wisdom in preparing and believing on behalf of your students, and may you experience healing in every aspect of your life. Amen.

CHAPTER 5

FOLLOW THE PATTERN

Key Idea: Rock-solid teachers use teaching patterns, experiences and activities to nurture life change.

When he had finished washing their feet, he put on his clothes and returned to his place. "Do you understand what I have done for you?" he asked them . . . "I have set you an example that you should do as I have done for you."

JOHN 13:12,15

Jeff, who teaches a Sunday School class of fifth and sixth graders, described his experience of watching a music video on TV: "In a three-and-a-half-minute video, the camera angles must have changed 53 times!

He continued, "I think about my students watching this video with so much input coming at them in so little time. Now, compare that to my Sunday School class, where I use one or two methods in an hour. No wonder we have trouble relating to kids!"

Jeff's thoughts highlight the teaching of the Master Teacher. How could Jesus keep crowds interested in His teaching for such long periods of time?

How Jesus Used Learning Experiences

Jesus involved His disciples in a special style of learning experiences. As rock-solid teachers, we can once again follow the Master Teacher's model. Consider three different aspects of learning situations: awareness, truth and experience.

Awareness

Awareness is when the student's motivation has been developed. The student hungers for the content of the lesson. Teaching for awareness occurs when you build the need in a student's life. Bruce Wilkinson states that when you build the need, you provide the main method of motivation in a student's life. This is our primary calling, because it brings the student's real need to the surface before we teach him or her the content.[1]

Truth

Truth is often the first aspect that comes to mind when we think of a biblically based learning situation. Truth means relating the story of God's relationship to people through His Word and communicating statements of doctrine that give life to learners. I call this the "true truth" that people naturally search for—"true truth" because "truth" is sometimes put in quotation marks in the postmodern world. By truth, we mean the rock-solid basis of teaching: "Your word is truth" (John 17:17).

Experience

Not all events are experience! Two words from the New Testament are translated "know:" One, *oida*, often means "to know as certainty"; the other, *ginosko*, means "to know in one's life." We'd use the word "experience" to describe the latter. This kind of knowledge comes from the street. It represents truth in shoe leather, learning from the school of reality. Teaching with experiences means helping students discern and interpret experience according to the standards of God's Word.

How Did Jesus Teach?

So what did Jesus do when He taught His disciples and other followers? Which type of learning did He use first? What order did He use when He approached learning experiences?

Truth, Experience, Awareness

A few times, Jesus began His teaching with truth, followed by experience and awareness. For example, His teaching on the resurrection followed this pattern: "He then began to teach them that the Son of Man must suffer many things and be rejected by the elders, chief priests and teachers of the law, and that he must be killed and after three days rise again" (Mark 8:31).

The apostle John provides this commentary about how Jesus' disciples later remembered what Jesus had taught:

> Jesus answered them, "Destroy this temple, and I will raise it again in three days." The Jews replied, "It has taken forty-six years to build this temple, and you are going to raise it in three days?" But the temple he had spoken of was his body. After he was raised from the dead, his disciples recalled what he had said. Then they believed the Scripture and the words that Jesus had spoken (John 2:19-22).

After Jesus' disciples experienced His death and resurrection, they had an awareness of what He'd taught.

Truth, Awareness, Experience

More often, Jesus began with truth and then followed it with awareness and experience. Jesus used this approach in the Sermon on the Mount. The truths that He gave us still echo in the spiritual life of believers.

First, Jesus spoke the truth about the Father's provision: "Do not worry about your life, what you will eat or drink; or about your body, what you will wear. Is not life more important than food, and the body more important than clothes?" (Matt. 6:25).

Jesus then helped the disciples become aware of the truth with illustrations of birds and flowers: "Look at the birds of the air; they do not sow or reap or store away in barns, and yet your heavenly Father feeds them . . . See how the lilies of the field grow. They do not labor or spin" (Matt. 6:26,28).

Finally, Jesus commanded the disciples to trust in God's provision: "Seek first his kingdom and his righteousness, and all these things will be given to you as well" (Matt. 6:33)—an exhortation for His followers to experience life change.

Experience, Awareness, Truth

Jesus most often taught by starting with experience and following it with awareness and truth. When Jesus taught the disciples to pray—what most of us grew up calling "The Lord's Prayer"—He followed this pattern (see Luke 11:1-4). He also used this pattern when He rebuked the disciples on the Sea of Galilee in order to stretch their faith (see Luke 8:25). And Jesus used this pattern when He fed the 5,000 as recorded in John 6:1-15—they ate (experience), they asked (awareness) and they believed (truth)!

Jesus used the same pattern with the woman at the well. First, Jesus requested a drink—the beginning of the experience for the woman (see John 4:7). Then came the awareness when she learned of living water: "If you knew the gift of God and who it is that asks you for a drink, you would have asked him and he would have given you living water" (John 4:10). And finally, the woman experienced truth when she expressed her faith in the Messiah: "The woman went back to the town and said to the people, 'Come, see a man who told me everything I ever did. Could this be the Christ?'" (vv. 28-29).

Perhaps the strongest example of this pattern occurs in John 13, where Jesus washed the disciples' feet (experience), had a discussion with Peter regarding the bathing of his whole body (awareness), and set an example of being a servant (truth).

Jesus had an incredible ability to take any experience and turn it into a learning situation. The technique of "guided conversation" follows the experience-awareness-truth pattern, as does the interactive learning model of teaching.

How Did Jesus Use Learning Activities?

As we use learning activities with our students, we cause our students to learn. What's so important about using learning activities? Jesus used learning activities for at least five purposes: motivational activities, orientation activities, information activities, application activities, and evaluation activities.[2]

Motivational Activities

The basic premise is this: Involvement motivates. This involves knowing our students' needs, characteristics, desires and knowledge—and developing experiences and activities that move them toward learning. (Chapter 6 lists many motivational activities that Jesus used as well as practical ideas that teachers today can try.)

Orientation Activities

When Jesus told the disciples to "put out into deep water, and let down the nets for a catch" (Luke 5:4), He was introducing an orientation learning activity. He used the activity to give them perspective about the starting point of being a disciple ("don't be afraid, from now on"), about where disciples should go ("you will catch men"), and the possible path to get there. Apparently, the disciples understood the lesson, because "they pulled their boats up on shore, left everything and followed him" (vv. 10-11).

When teachers use learning activities in their lessons, the following occur:

- *A perspective or understanding about the learner's starting point is gained.* For example, teenagers often want to know how a lesson applies to them. This is the principle of "meaningfulness."

- *An objective or future outcome to be achieved is obtained.* Even children like to know what is expected. This is the principle of "direction."

- *A course of action is set in the early part of the learning situation.* This is the principle of "next step."

Information Activities

Jesus used learning activities to teach people basic information. For example, Jesus used the illustration of the coin to teach about paying taxes (see Luke 20:24-25), the transfiguration to teach about His deity (see Matt. 17:1-9), the example of the child to teach about true greatness (see Luke 9:46-48), the healing of the man with the withered hand to teach about the forgiveness of sin (see Mark 3:1-5).

Teachers can teach information by using creative-writing pieces (letter writing, poetry, diaries, and so forth), field trips, puppets, role-playing, interviews, case studies or art (posters, finger paints, collages, cartooning). You don't have to feel stuck in a rut. Creative interactive learning methods might teach students even more than traditional methods.

Application Activities

The intent of an application activity is to help students recall a principle and use it in a situation. Jesus used application learning activities when He went to Lazarus's tomb (see John 11:17-44), when He told the disciples to cast the net on the other side of the boat (see John 21:6), and when He fed the 5,000 (see Luke 9:10-17).

Veteran children's ministry leader Barbara Bolton states, "Changed lives occur as a work of the Holy Spirit when the learner is actively involved in the process of applying Scripture to life experiences."[3] Children should be given the opportunity to practice what they learn so they can remember it when they go home. Teenagers might "present the gospel" in class so they're ready to share at school. Adults who practice a personal quiet time in a small group will know how to do it on their own at home. Our families provide an ideal place to practice what we preach in many areas, including media selection, learning to give encouragement, and engaging in positive conversation.

Evaluation Activities

Jesus used evaluation activities to help learners gauge where they were in their own faith, such as when the sinful woman anointed His feet with expensive perfume (see Luke 7:36-50). Jesus used such activities to help people understand servant leadership and forgiveness of sins, and to help them recognize His deity.

Summary and evaluation activities are essential for our learners. Children might draw pictures of how to be helpful at home. Teenagers can role-play the extension of forgiveness to a friend. Adults might plan a presentation about how Jesus is God.

Putting Jesus' Use of Learning Experiences into Practice

We've touched briefly on ways to use some of these activities and experiences. Let's look at some other practical ways that rock-solid teachers can use teaching patterns, experience and activities to foster life change in their students.

With Children

- *Plan for the children to have fun!* This is one of the five foundational principles of the Awana Clubs International ministry. Children often learn more through play than through more formal education. They don't need constant, breathless activity to experience meaningful learning. But you can use unique games and activities to draw children into a lesson, to give them opportunities to enjoy participating in class, and to prepare them for learning. A growing number of educators recommend godly play to enhance learning in a child's life.[4]

- *Use Bible learning activities:*

  □ Tell the purpose of the activity.
  □ Give clear directions.
  □ Let children work at their own pace.
  □ Use guided conversation.
  □ Summarize what was learned.
  □ Share the learning with others.[5]

With Youth

- *Prepare teens to learn from the moment they enter the classroom.* Use music, activities, hospitality hosts and contact information/registration material to show students that you welcome and value them.

- *Tap into the resource of the students themselves.* Most teenagers demonstrate a high motivation to learn through activity, so develop student leaders by putting them in charge of directing the learning activities of your youth group (with a little guidance). Don't underestimate the value of having teens involved in other church ministries.

- *Employ some of these learning experiences:*

  □ Hands down, hands up: In prayers of confession, agree with the Lord about your sin (hands palm down on your lap), then turn your hands over or raise your hands to ask for power and filling from the Holy Spirit.

□ Discipline of silence: Lead the youth group in a discipline of silence retreat. Students spend quiet time alone with the Lord with a Bible, a pen and an outline. When I've used this experience, the schedule included:

- *Focus time.* Get in touch with the Lord by reading several psalms (try Psalms 1; 19; 139).
- *Adoration:* Honor the Lord through worship. Sing to Him and praise Him for His character and work in your life. Use the letters of the alphabet to shape your praise of God's character.
- *Confession:* Agree with God about your sins. Let Him reveal areas you need to change or to ask His forgiveness. Don't forget to thank Him for forgiving you (see Pss. 32; 51; 1 John 1).
- *Thanksgiving:* Give thanks for the Lord's work in your own life, your family, your church, your school, your country and your world.
- *Supplication:* Make your requests known to the Lord Jesus in these same areas.
- *Sharing time.* Get together with others in your group to share from your written highlights.

□ Implement prayer groups: When I led a youth group, the teenagers wanted to have extended prayer groups led by the students themselves. So we started B.R.I.D.G.E. (Being Responsible In Discipling God's Elect). These times became the highlight of our Wednesday night meetings. We simply assigned two "shepherds" (usually a girl and a guy for each group of 10 students) to do three things: (1) contact each group member every week via phone, e-mail or in person; (2) pray for and with each student—usually during the youth-group meeting; and (3) seek to meet whatever spiritual needs they discerned.

With Adults

• *Use appropriate Bible learning activities.* When I was a young youth pastor, I directed a group of senior adults to make posters for their Sunday School class on the floor of the sanctuary. One of the men asked, "Pastor, is there anything else you want me to do when I get down there? At my age, it might take a while to get up!"

• *Train adult classes to try learning activities.* Often, adults are really bored in class, but they either don't know anything different or are too polite to tell their teachers. One teacher gathered a bunch of clothing and other items to create a situation in which the young adult students would experience what it was like to have physical limitations as senior adults. During the class, students had to wear and use items such as gloves, thick sweaters, large shoes, bulky pants, earplugs and high-powered glasses.

With Your Family

• *Participate (or help start) a Family Together Sunday School class in your church.*[6] One class's leadership team set up four to six learning centers every week for participating family members to enjoy the following:

  □ *Refreshments:* a must in some Christian education circles
  □ *Literature:* handing out the *Family Walk* devotional the class used
  □ *Games:* some active, others not so much, but all tied to the theme of the day
  □ *Music:* using this important medium to prepare and enhance learning
  □ *Equipping activities:* to practice at church what families would later do at home

- *Watch cartoons (or other TV programs) as a family.* This can be a fantastic learning experience. Here's what happens:

  - You become aware of the worldview aimed toward your child.
  - You might actually have fun with your children—just spending time together creates positive memories.
  - You can model how to believe or respond to a statement or event in a program. I call this "talking back to the TV." It provides a frame of reference for children that will serve them well when you're not around.

- *Plan a directed learning activity.* When one of our sons made fun of a student in the special education program at school, we put together a directed learning activity for our family. Donna and I set a course of learning that included:

  - Blindfolds for a half hour, along with guided conversation about my cousin, who married a blind man
  - Not using their legs for a half hour
  - Using earplugs for a half hour
  - Not being able to use their arms for a half hour

As we sought to teach our boys about disabilities, the experiences prompted great discussion. In addition, one son became a peer mentor for a mentally handicapped child later that year.

Self-Check

Before you turn to chapter 6, take a few minutes to evaluate how you're fulfilling your role as a rock-solid teacher in the area of using teaching patterns, experiences and activities in your teaching. Just between you and God, rate how you're doing at using these tools to move your students toward life change. Spend some time in prayer asking God to help you grow in areas in which you're struggling.

I follow the patterns that Jesus used, not allowing the experience to be dismissed from my teaching.

strongly agree   *agree*   *not sure*   *disagree*   *strongly disagree*

I create learning experiences that have variety and meaning.

strongly agree   *agree*   *not sure*   *disagree*   *strongly disagree*

I regularly assess my students to see which method will work best in teaching them.

strongly agree   *agree*   *not sure*   *disagree*   *strongly disagree*

I'm a continual learner.

strongly agree   *agree*   *not sure*   *disagree*   *strongly disagree*

I believe in trying new ways to impact those whom I instruct.

strongly agree   *agree*   *not sure*   *disagree*   *strongly disagree*

Benediction

May the creativity of the Master Teacher and the awareness of the Holy Spirit's motivation be evident in the response to the truth in the lives of those whom you teach.

CHAPTER 6

MOTIVATE TO LEARN

Key Idea: Rock-solid teachers are catalysts for change in the lives of their students.

When he saw the crowds, he had compassion on them, because they were harassed and helpless, like sheep without a shepherd.

MATTHEW 9:36

Andrew, Simon Peter's brother, was one of the two who heard what John had said and who had followed Jesus. The first thing Andrew did was to find his brother Simon and tell him, "We have found the Messiah" (that is, the Christ). And he brought him to Jesus.

JOHN 1:40-42

I listened as a teacher tried to explain the characteristics of God to a group of fifth graders. One by one, he pulled prepared items—21 to be exact—out of a large paper bag. He asked the students how each item represented God: "How is God like a candy bar?" "How is God like a comb?" and so forth.

With each question, I became more concerned. Then I glanced at the other leaders, who just looked confused! And what did the students get at the end of the lesson? Leftover items that the teacher gave away after he used them to explain God.

I wish I could have chatted with this teacher about the way kids learn before he went to all that work. I wish he'd known about what motivates and connects with preteen students before he became so discouraged at the way they responded.

What Motivates Students?

By examining the way Jesus viewed and interacted with people, we can discover a lot about what naturally motivates the students we teach.

Students are curious. In his Gospel, Matthew noted that crowds of people flocked to see Jesus and to hear Him teach. Often, they were dealing with all the stresses of life: "they were harassed and helpless" (Matt. 9:36). But as a wise instructor, Jesus used their natural curiosity and their situations in life to cause them to learn.

Students are "depraved." What does it mean to be depraved? Spiritually, this term signifies our total bankruptcy before God. Without the Holy Spirit prompting us, we have no understanding of God. Because we aren't "good" in our innermost being, we'll naturally turn aside (see Rom. 3:10-11). The prophet Isaiah described why we need a Savior: "We all, like sheep, have gone astray, each of us has turned to his own way; and the LORD has laid on him the iniquity of us all" (Isa. 53:6).

God loves students. Matthew also pointed out that Jesus had compassion on the crowds who came to listen to Him. Perhaps it's the most repeated truth we hear as Christians, but it's still true: God really does love each of us.

Students have physical needs. Jesus sought to provide for His learners so that their thinking and learning wouldn't be hindered. When the disciples wanted the crowd to go find food for themselves, Jesus said, "They do not need to go away. You give them something to eat" (Matt. 14:16). When our students are hungry, tired or distracted in any way, we'll always have to work harder to motivate them.

Students can think rationally and critically. Just like the disciples who listened to Jesus and followed Him (see John 1:37), students today can come up with profound insights. It just takes a presentation of sound information, the influence and work of the Holy Spirit, and the students' own reasoning.

Students have social needs. The disciples who followed Jesus approached Him in pairs. When they heard about Jesus, they immediately went and found close family members to tell about the experience. Don't you wish you had a whole herd of motivated Andrews to participate in outreach from your class? I like the way Ohio State University education professor Anita Woolfolk describes this educational concept: "To learn is to participate in the life of the community. . . . In other words, we learn by the company we keep."[1]

Students can respond and change. Students of all ages are more than just capable of obeying God themselves—they can also help others to know, love and serve Christ! The first disciples did this immediately: "The first thing Andrew did was to find his brother Simon and tell him, 'We have found the Messiah' (that is, the Christ). And he brought him to Jesus" (John 1:41-42).

I remember Alice, a teenager who came to our youth group, who heard the gospel and accepted Christ. Later, we learned that she had been pretty messed up because of drugs and a promiscuous lifestyle. During the next few whirlwind weeks, she explained her new life to her mom, reached out to her old friends, started a new life in Christ, and witnessed to anyone who would listen.

Students of all ages are capable of response and change. And they can lead others to know Christ and grow in Him.

Practical Ways to Use Student Motivation

The principles we just discussed describe how Jesus viewed and interacted with students. But how did He motivate people to learn? Let's use the letters of the alphabet to examine how Jesus created a learning response in the lives of His followers and the practical ways that we, as rock-solid teachers, can best use those motivations.

A-Attitude

Jesus ministered to the hearts of people. He dealt with their attitudes and was influenced by their emotions. We should always try to be aware of our students' attitudes when we teach. When we avoid them, we decrease our students' motivation.

A 15-year-old in my youth group was excited to discover that "Jesus wept!" (John 11:35). It deepened his understanding that Jesus really cared about the emotions, concerns and sadness in people.

We can divide the ways we influence students into three areas: cognitive (thinking), affective (attitude) and response (doing). The area that most teachers neglect is attitude. Because this area includes the affection of love, it might be the most important of the three. We all need a greater awareness of Jesus' greatest commandment (see Mark 12:29-31), for then we will have a more holistic approach to students and remember that they are individuals who both think *and* feel.

B-Begin Well

When Jesus is first introduced, John the Baptist—a respected prophet—"sponsored" Him (John 1:35-36). In addition, Jesus was clear, intentional and winsome when He called His first disciples (see Matt. 4:18-22).

Our teaching times should begin with connecting with our students. Just as with the opening credits of a movie or a TV show, we often best remember what comes first and what comes last. This is called "primacy and recency."

To begin well, try some of these lesson-approach ideas:

- Tell a story.
- Sing a song related to your theme.
- Use humor.
- Develop interest centers: missions, age-appropriate literature, music or games.

- Show a picture, graphic or other overhead.
- Use skits, drama or readings.
- Work on an art project together.
- Give a test.
- Have the students do some creative writing.
- Do a puppet presentation.[2]

C-Cooperation

Jesus rebuked His disciples when they became exclusive. "'Master,' said John, 'we saw a man driving out demons in your name and we tried to stop him, because he is not one of us.' 'Do not stop him,' Jesus said, 'for whoever is not against you is for you'" (Luke 9:49-50).

Encouraging cooperation in your students enhances their motivation. At times, you can also use competition, but a cooperative atmosphere usually motivates students better. In fact, the best competition involves students working together to compete against a goal instead of against each other. Competition motivates best when it provides opportunity for the cooperative success of many students instead of just a gifted few.

D-Discipline

Discipline motivates by giving students instruction (knowledge of what is expected), by giving them training (the ability to *practice* without being put down for not being perfect), and by giving them correction (changing attitude and behavior when it hinders learning). Some effective methods for discipline include:

- *Instruction*. This aspect of discipline comes from the same idea as being a "disciple." It means to be a learner.

- *Training*. Just knowing the right thing to do isn't enough. Students also need to be trained how to do it. Just as athletes train physically for the Olympics, we need to move students beyond knowing the right thing to do spiritually and help them understand the value of spiritual training. As the apostle Paul advised, "For physical training is of some value, but godliness has value for all things, holding promise for both the present life and the life to come" (1 Tim. 4:8).

- *Correction.* Teachers and parents usually jump directly to correction when they're concerned about a student's motivation. Wise teachers make sure they try instruction and training first. Correction then makes sense to the student.

E-Encouragement

Provide encouragement to your students to motivate them to do their best. Jesus demonstrated these practical steps when He encouraged the churches in Revelation:

1. *He knew their situation.* Jesus used reassuring words such as "I know your afflictions and your poverty—yet you are rich! I know the slander . . . Do not be afraid of what you are about to suffer . . . He who overcomes will not be hurt at all by the second death to help the Smyrna church understand that He understood their situation" (Rev. 2:9-11).

2. *He took action steps.* Notice that Jesus included the steps of reward, patience and opportunity as parts of His encouragement: "I will give you the crown of life" (Rev. 2:10); "I have given her time to repent of her immorality, but she is unwilling" (v. 21); "See, I have placed before you an open door that no one can shut" (3:8).

3. *He provided encouragement through exhortation, resource, reassurance and reward.* Jesus said, "He who has an ear, let him hear what the Spirit says to the churches. He who overcomes will not be hurt at all by the second death" (Rev. 2:11).

Encouragement is like jet fuel when it comes to motivating students. I once had a middle school student in our youth group who required some special attention. As I worked with this student, I realized that he had some needs that we could address through some discipleship steps. This included having an accountability time with the student right before our meeting time each Wednesday night. After this student had grown through this process for a month, he began helping with the group's opening prayer time.

If we want motivated students, we need to encourage them to give their best efforts.

F-Friend of Sinners

Jesus' enemies attached this label to Him (see Matt. 11:19). But what a great way to describe exactly who Jesus is!

People who already have a relationship with the Savior must also be a friend of sinners by befriending those who still need to know Him. When you're a friend to people who need friends, you motivate both them and yourself. You can accomplish this in a practical way by making sure you greet anyone who visits your class, by making sure that visitors provide contact information for you to follow up, and by making sure that visitors are shown hospitality and acceptance in your group.

G-Guidance

Jesus gave specific instructions for His disciples as they prepared for an evangelistic campaign in Galilee:

> Take nothing for the journey—no staff, no bag, no bread, no money, no extra tunic. Whatever house you enter, stay there until you leave that town. If people do not welcome you, shake the dust off your feet when you leave their town, as a testimony against them (Luke 9:3-5).

As teachers, we need to make sure we're providing specific instructions to our students—especially when they are tackling something new. "Guiding" or "shepherding" means giving our students advice, supervision, direction and support to make good choices. You might find yourself providing specific procedures for students to follow, sharing your expectations, or guiding them about what to do if they don't understand something.

H-Humor

Some people are surprised to learn that Jesus had a sense of humor. He never put down others, but He often brought out the humorous aspects of life. Typically, His humor was subtle, as seen in His story of the blind leading the blind: "If a blind man leads a blind man, both will fall into a pit" (Matt. 15:14).

It's almost impossible to not like someone who makes you laugh. Appropriate humor can be a good way to motivate students to act. Spend time at a local bookstore or at humor sites on the Internet, reading jokes and scanning for humorous stories that you can use in your teaching. Funny situations exist all around you, so observe what happens to others, as well as the humorous circumstances in your own life.

I-Intercession

Jesus prayed often: "Very early in the morning, while it was still dark, Jesus got up, left the house and went off to a solitary place, where he prayed" (Mark 1:35). He prayed for His disciples (see John 17:6-19), with His disciples (see Luke 11:1-4), and He urged His disciples to also pray—as in the Garden of Gethsemane (see Mark 14:32-38).

Pray for fresh ways to motivate your students. Pray for their learning and for their obedience to follow what God teaches them. I remember struggling to lead one youth group. I began meeting with one of the church's leaders, and together we prayed specifically for members of the youth group. I was surprised at how much these teenagers changed! Maybe they changed as the Lord answered our prayers. Or maybe I changed. Or maybe both! Regardless, I learned that prayer can motivate.

J-Just As They Are

Jesus accepts us with all of our needs. The apostle Paul urged us to treat others the same way Jesus treats us: "Accept one another, then, just as Christ accepted you, in order to bring praise to God" (Rom. 15:7).

Accept your students just as they are and lift them to where God wants them to be. Students will be motivated by an inviting, accepting teacher who mentors them toward the Lord.

K-Knowledge

Jesus knew His disciples intimately. He gained much of this knowledge through prayer (see Luke 6:12-13). Yet despite knowing all of their faults, weaknesses and sins, Jesus "loved them to the end" (John 13:1, *NKJV*).

Know as much as you can about your students—their names, their daily activities, and their prayer requests. As you get to know your students better and they grow to trust you, you'll increase their motivation to learn more about the Lord.

L-Learning Styles

Jesus seemed to be aware of various learning styles when He taught. His teaching included auditory methods (sermons), visual methods (illustrations and demonstrations) and active methods (washing in the pool of Siloam; see John 9:7). He taught so that people with every learning style had the opportunity to learn.

As a teacher, try to accommodate various learning styles—even those that don't reflect how you learn. Marlene LeFever provides excellent observations on learning styles: First, Jesus taught with such variety and intentionality that He met the needs of students with each style. Second, if we want to imitate Jesus' teaching, we need to learn about different learning styles, practice teaching in ways that are outside of our comfort zone, and aim to improve continuously.[3]

M-Meaningfulness

When Jesus dealt with the Pharisees, He started with what they knew and moved to the unknown: "You diligently study the Scriptures because you think that by them you possess eternal life. These are the Scriptures that testify about me" (John 5:39). He stressed the motivating principle of meaningfulness. He also used meaningfulness when dealing with a positive Pharisee, Nicodemus. As recorded in John 3:8, Jesus described the wind (the known) to bring understanding about the Spirit's work (the unknown).

Meaningfulness provides two applications for motivation: (1) we learn when we move from the known to the unknown; and (2) we make application to life when we take what we know and make it meaningful to daily living and faith.

People want to learn things that apply to them. This means that your teaching needs to make sense in how it connects to your students' lives. How is what you're teaching meaningful? Lawrence Richards and Gary Bredfeldt put it simply: "People learn best when learning is relevant."[4] Steven Yelon, professor emeritus of educational psychology at Michigan State University, offers these ideas to make teaching more meaningful for students:

- Relate what you're teaching to a strong interest that students already have.
- Provide a real problem to start your lesson.
- Connect the lesson to practical ways the students can use what they're learning.
- Use meaningful quotes.
- Tell how others have successfully applied the lesson.
- Point out likely problems that will occur if students don't apply the ideas you present.
- Conduct an activity that demonstrates the need to apply the lesson.
- Ask a question to show how the students need the content of the lesson.
- Present an unsolved case and encourage students to offer ideas about how to bring the situation to an appropriate conclusion.
- Contrast students' various beliefs, actions and perspectives.[5]

N-Needs

Jesus met people's needs, including their need for food, safety and a sense of belonging and purpose.

If we want to motivate students by meeting their needs, we need to know what those needs are. Ask your students questions. Develop a simple survey for children, teenagers or parents to complete. Check out what experts (those who work with students in educational and works settings) are saying in books, magazines and other media about the needs of people like those you teach.

O-Overview

Jesus knew where His learners were (see John 2:24). He always knew how to please His Father in heaven (see John 8:29). Jesus then taught in specific "next steps" that each disciple could obey.

One of the best ways you can get an overview of where your students are involves asking three questions (note that steps 1 and 2 are interchangeable):

1. Where do we want to go?
2. Where are we?
3. What is the next step?

When I'm at a loss to motivate a particular student or group, I often fall back on this motivational tool. I try to assess where the student or group should be, and then try to determine where they are and what next step they should take.

P-Planning

Even Jesus planned. At times, He set the curriculum of a learning situation, such as when He demonstrated a resolute will and determination by setting His face to go to Jerusalem (see Luke 9:51) or when He ministered to the woman at the well in Samaria in an intentional way (see John 4:1-38). Other times, Jesus allowed the student to set the agenda (see Mark 12:28). Either way, He was prepared to cause the student to learn.

Further, Jesus also knew how to plan what *not* to teach. Jesus said, "I still have many things to say to you, but you cannot bear them now" (John 16:12, *NKJV*). As teachers, we can plan learning situations that won't overwhelm learners or leave them unmotivated.

Q-Quiet

Sometimes Jesus changed the pace for His disciples. When they needed rest or time away from the crowds, Jesus provided it, saying to the disciples,

"Come with me by yourselves to a quiet place" (Mark 6:31).

As teachers, we need to cue students when to be quiet and reflect. These times of quiet renew and ready students for new learning and can help them develop insight and commitment. Build in quiet reflection time for your class times of worship, learning and service.

As teachers, we also need times of quiet and reflection for our own motivation—spiritual retreats and time away from ministry. I encourage teachers who work together in a club or in a Sunday School ministry to practice an extended time of prayer. This involves devoting several hours to praying alone in the same location and then gathering together to share and pray together. These can be great times for team-building and receiving direction from the Lord.

R-Relationships

Jesus built rock-solid relationships at various levels of intimacy. One disciple, John, was very close to Jesus. He even referred to himself as "the disciple whom Jesus loved" (John 21:7). Jesus also involved three of His disciples in special leadership training: worship on the Mount of Transfiguration (see Mark 9:2-13), raising Jairus's daughter from the dead (see Luke 8:49-56), and praying in the Garden of Gethsemane (see Mark 14:32-42).

Jesus selected 12 disciples: "He appointed twelve—designating them apostles—that they might be with him and that he might send them out to preach" (Mark 3:14). Beyond the Twelve, Jesus had the Seventy and multitudes upon multitudes of people to whom He ministered.

Jesus moved among these relationships with such ease that it is easy to miss the group dynamic if we aren't observing carefully. He adjusted the number of people according to the goal He wanted to accomplish.

What do groups have to do with motivating students? Different levels of relationship existed in Jesus' life. He didn't exclude anyone but ministered to everyone at appropriate levels. He knew when to be with a few individuals and focus on their needs. He also knew when to transition and meet the needs of many.

As teachers, we have to practice and adjust to make group dynamics easier for our students. We can help them develop relationships by moving between individual relationships, small groups and large groups.

S-Success

Jesus defined success for His followers. Sometimes, their fear of failing held them back from obeying Jesus. He gave them confidence, forgave them when they failed, and commissioned them to new levels of service.

In the book of Revelation, Jesus modeled how to motivate students with success:

- *Jesus started out with positive statements about the seven churches he addressed.* He commended Ephesus on their hard work, perseverance and testing of the false teachers (see 2:2-3). Each of the churches received positive commendation, except Laodicea.

- *Jesus then addressed the areas in which the churches needed improvement.* "Yet I hold this against you: You have forsaken your first love" (2:4). He motivated two of the churches without saying anything that needed improvement!

- *Jesus made more encouraging statements than ones of rebuke.* For example, He said three or four very commendable characteristics about the church in Ephesus, and then listed only one area but a very important one in which the church could grow (see 2:1-4).

Jesus outlined the steps of obedience and exhorted the church in Ephesus to take those steps: "Remember the height from which you have fallen! Repent and do the things you did at first. If you do not repent, I will come to you and remove your lampstand from its place" (2:5). Jesus also gave the wayward church of Laodicea ample invitation to restore their dependency upon the Lord and enjoy fellowship with Him (see 3:20).

What about our teaching? How can we take specific steps to motivate with success?

- *Start with the positive.* When you correct a student, start with what they've done right. When you evaluate how instruction went, write down five positives before you begin to describe what a student could improve. Fear of failure holds many students back. Some won't try new things because they think their effort won't be good enough.

- *Don't hold back from correction when it's needed.* Most of us don't need help to see students that need to move from failure. But do we make a successful outcome obvious? Often we spend a lot of time recounting what's wrong, but do we describe what right behavior and success look like?

- *Notice the positive/negative ratio.* We should spend much more time in positive reinforcement (describing how success might look) than in negative reinforcement (outlining what's wrong with behavior, responses or attitudes). This is grace in action.

Establish the basis of a right relationship for the future. When a student knows specific action steps and has been encouraged by a teacher to take those steps, real learning can then take place. That's teaching for success.

T-Two by Two

The Lord Jesus sent out the Seventy to minister in pairs (see Luke 10:1). If we don't look closely, we can lose the significance of this tactic. Pairs provide safety, flexibility, cross-training and additional insight. Jesus knew that by sending out His followers in pairs or small groups, they'd experience fellowship, support and strength.

For teachers, a practical application involves teaching in pairs and in teams. Experts sometimes recommend that club and Sunday School ministries think of student-teacher ratios not in one teacher for every year of age of the students, plus one, but rather in two or more teachers with the appropriate student ratio.

This provides greater safety for the ministry (as in child-protection policies). But the real benefits include class continuity, cross-training of workers, training new workers and bearing the burden of the ministry together.

U-Understanding

Although Jesus didn't neglect potential learners, He did test their commitment and openness to learn (for example, see John 6). Jesus provided the choice for people to follow Him or not. As Christian education author Lawrence Richards notes, "Understanding is a moral and spiritual issue, not an intellectual one."[6]

As teachers, we need to determine whether our students are ready to learn as well as the moral nature of the choices they make. Often, we give most of our attention to students who cause problems, leaving on their own those who are motivated to learn.

When I was just starting out in youth ministry, a pastor advised me, "Move with the movers!" In other words, set a positive model with students who want to learn and then move to work with those who are less responsive.

V-Visit Your Students

Jesus often went to visit those He taught: Simon the Leper (see Mark 14:3), the Samaritan village (see John 4:40) and Zacchaeus (see Luke 19:5). Of course, you'll need to use care when doing visitation. Never visit by yourself—the two-by-two principle certainly applies here.

Although some children's ministries have stopped trying to build relationships through visitation, I know of one church that emphasizes getting to know the students and their parents. This relational aspect built outside of class results in an effective outreach to entire families. Another Sunday School teacher I know hosts a picnic at the end of each summer for her entire class and their families. You can use creative forms of visitation to motivate students.

W-Weigh the Motives

Jesus focused mainly on people's internal issues. In fact, that's why He often clashed with the Pharisees. He said, "You Pharisees clean the outside of the cup and dish, but inside you are full of greed and wickedness" (Luke 11:39), meaning they paid attention to how things looked rather than what really motivated behavior from within. Jesus said, "Nothing outside a man can make him 'unclean' by going into him. Rather, it is what comes out of a man that makes him 'unclean'" (Mark 7:15).

I've worked with students who don't think they control their own learning. They point to the teacher, circumstances or other students for why they can't learn. But the best learning takes place internally.

Educational experts describe the source of a student's motivation as the "locus of causality,"[7] a term that describes whether the source is internal or external. When a student complies because of outside influence, it's called extrinsic motivation. That's not bad—it just has limitations. As a child grows, the goal is to see the motivation from learning shift to internal sources.

I have a friend whose 17-year-old son has trouble organizing his history notebook for a grade, yet has no trouble organizing the equipment, music and personnel for a performance at a school assembly or community fair. That's because organizing the notebook is only an external source of motivation, while music—being his passion—provides an internal source of motivation. Motivation for some students involves weighing the motives.

X-X Factor (the Unknown)

Jesus revealed the unknown: "No one has ever seen God, but God the One and Only, who is at the Father's side, has made him known" (John 1:18). He also moved from what His listeners knew (in parables) to reveal the unknown (heavenly truths).

Revealing the unknown increases students' curiosity. Teaching is an "incarnational" ministry. In other words, the only Jesus some students will see is through you. Motivating them might hinge on finding Jesus in the midst of mundane things. So you might spend time praying that the little responses of your teaching will reflect the deep love of Christ for your students.

As teachers, we can restart our students' love of learning. This happens when we review old things from a new viewpoint or show our excitement about new discoveries. I know a youth pastor who learned to skateboard, surf and play computer games because, as he discipled the teens in his group, he also asked them to teach him something he didn't know.

Y-Yearning

Jesus demonstrated great compassion for the people He taught. When He viewed Jerusalem, He lamented, "How often I have longed to gather your children together, as a hen gathers her chicks under her wings, but you were not willing" (Matt. 23:37).

As teachers, we need to yearn for life change in the lives of our students by using the tools of prayer, observation and interaction. Students want to be wanted! This means demonstrating our compassion for them in tangible ways—greeting them by name, listening to them, praying for and with them, and so on. We need the same kind of yearning that Paul had to see people come to the Lord (see Rom. 9:1-3).

Z-Zeal

Jesus demonstrated enthusiasm for His teaching. When He cleansed the Temple, "His disciples remembered that it was written: 'Zeal for your house will consume me'" (John 2:17).

Zeal is contagious! Notify your face and demeanor about the enthusiasm that you have inside of you for the Lord. Be passionate about what you want to teach. Enthusiasm comes from a word that means "in God." So, who should be more enthusiastic than Christian teachers?

I once was getting ready to share at a seminar and discovered that the PowerPoint projector wouldn't function. So I decided to open my Bible, teach as best I could, and not worry about the nifty visuals I'd planned. As I fired a prayer to the Lord to help me be creative and communicative, I decided to just share what was on my heart. Some of the participants told me afterward that it was the best seminar they had been to in years. I went away realizing that zeal can motivate!

Putting Jesus' Method of Motivating Students into Practice

As rock-solid teachers, we can use the ways Jesus motivated students. Here are some specific ideas.

With Children

- *Use guided conversation.* This skill encompasses many of these motivators. You touch on attitude, discipline, encouragement, meaningfulness and relationship during guided conversation. Use these suggestions for guided conversation:

    □ Guided conversation is informal but planned dialogue.
    □ We usually give more thought to the things we say to children in conveying knowledge; our words are even more potent in conveying attitudes.
    □ The relationship or attitude we build will have great impact on the learning a child will do.
    □ Accept feelings.
    □ Accept ideas.
    □ Offer praise and encouragement.
    □ Ask open-ended questions.[8]

With Youth

- *Use humor to motivate teenagers.* You can say things in good-natured humor that you could never get away with in direct speech.

- *Ask students to pray for you.* I know one youth leader who tells his class, "If you won't pray, then I won't teach!"

With Adults

- *Take adult leaders on a "cruise of motivating factors."* Essentially, this means conducting a review of the material in this chapter.

With Your Own Family

- *Employ the success principle.* Donna and I realized during a family evening that we were saying no a lot. We actually were playing switch the roles, meaning that our boys became the parents and the parents became the children. So we decided to speak commendations to each of our sons before we spoke correction. We even declared a moratorium on corrective statements for a week. We were surprised how these positive statements motivated our sons: "Thank you for taking out the garbage" replaced "You haven't taken out the trash."

• *Be zealous—make sure you practice what you preach.* This can motivate your children and can help to eliminate the hypocrisy gap.

Self-Check

Before you turn to chapter 7, take a few minutes to evaluate how you're fulfilling your role as a rock-solid teacher in the area of using the way students are naturally motivated. Just between you and God, rate how you're doing at teaching in this area. Spend some time in prayer asking God to help you grow in areas in which you're struggling.

I study students to know their needs, characteristics, desires and knowledge.

strongly agree　　　*agree*　　　*not sure*　　　*disagree*　　　*strongly disagree*

I prepare lessons from biblical content with a view to motivate students to learn.

strongly agree　　　*agree*　　　*not sure*　　　*disagree*　　　*strongly disagree*

My goal is to increase my observation and understanding of my students so that I can do my part to motivate them for Christ.

strongly agree　　　*agree*　　　*not sure*　　　*disagree*　　　*strongly disagree*

I regularly review motivational principles in my own life and in the lives of those I teach.

strongly agree　　　*agree*　　　*not sure*　　　*disagree*　　　*strongly disagree*

I begin my lessons with planned activity to motivate my students from where they are in life to a place where they can take a step of obedience.
strongly agree   *agree*   *not sure*   *disagree*   *strongly disagree*

I build relationships with students through activities such as encouragement, friendship, intercession and visitation.
strongly agree   *agree*   *not sure*   *disagree*   *strongly disagree*

I employ discipline and guidance in my class to motivate my students.
strongly agree   *agree*   *not sure*   *disagree*   *strongly disagree*

I seek to bring meaning to the learning situation through knowledge of my students and their learning styles.
strongly agree   *agree*   *not sure*   *disagree*   *strongly disagree*

I employ both humor and quietness in appropriate ways while teaching.
strongly agree   *agree*   *not sure*   *disagree*   *strongly disagree*

Benediction

May the Lord Jesus Christ give you insight into your own motivations and send you out to be a catalyst for Him in drawing students into an exciting, motivated obedience. Amen.

CHAPTER 7

KNOW THE SCRIPTURES

Key Idea: Rock-solid teachers work to grasp the content of God's Word and help students apply it.

Jesus answered and said to them, "Are you not therefore mistaken, because you do not know the Scriptures nor the power of God?"

MARK 12:24, *NKJV*

They asked each other, "Were not our hearts burning within us while he talked with us on the road and opened the Scriptures to us?"

LUKE 24:32

Jay, one of the leaders at a midweek club meeting, asked me to sit in while he taught so that I could give him some feedback. We planned to talk over a decaf mocha at a nearby coffee shop after the club meeting ended.

I'm not sure if Jay was concerned that I was listening or if he just wanted to finish up on time, but as the students worked on their memory verses, Jay announced, "Don't worry about the meaning—just get the verse done!" I couldn't believe my ears!

Guess what Jay and I chatted about over coffee? You guessed it. Gently, I urged Jay to make sure his students didn't simply recite verses but that they understood the meaning of the words. I suggested that he explain why God included the verses in Scripture, ask the students what they thought the verses meant, and then encourage the students to figure out ways they could use the verses.

No matter what age your students are, this is a common problem. But our goal as teachers should be to help our students get to *know* the Bible. We should move them toward obeying the Lord.

Knowing the Scriptures is where we start. It can't be where we *end*!

Knowing and Obeying God's Word

As we noted in chapter 5, two words from the Greek New Testament are translated "know." One, *oida*, often means "to know as certainty." The other, *ginosko*, often means "to know in experience." To grasp the content of Scripture, we need to involve both meanings of knowing in our teaching process.

Teachers must start with the Scriptures. Our students don't need to just know the Word, but they also need to learn how to obey. And how do students live according to the Bible? By applying what it teaches. So let's look at how both we and our students can understand and apply God's Word.

How Did Jesus View Scripture?

During Jesus' earthly ministry, He modeled how we should view Scripture.

Jesus memorized passages. When Jesus was tempted in the wilderness by Satan, He used passages from Scripture three times to resist the temptation.

It is written: "Man does not live on bread alone, but on every word that comes from the mouth of God . . . It is also written: "Do not put the Lord your God to the test" . . . Away from me, Satan! For it is written: "Worship the Lord your God, and serve him only" (Matt. 4:4,7,10).

In addition to urging our students to memorize Scripture, we should be doing the same ourselves. Do you memorize portions of God's Word? Don't be someone who communicates to students, "Do as I say, but not as I do!"

Jesus preached from the Scriptures. Jesus used Old Testament prophecies to invite people to believe in Him (see Luke 4:17-22). What sources do you use for lessons when you teach? Do you use actual Scripture passages, or do you just focus on sharing your own ideas that might be vaguely biblical?

Jesus viewed the Bible as authoritative. Jesus also used Old Testament prophecies to show the truth of God's Word and taught that the prophecies must be fulfilled: "The scripture cannot be broken" (John 10:35, KJV). Do you lead your students to submit to the authority of God's Word? Again, don't forget about yourself: Are you submitting to God's teaching?

Jesus taught scriptural truth. Jesus used the instruction of Scripture to help His disciples understand His teachings: "Beginning with Moses and all the Prophets, he explained to them what was said in all the Scriptures concerning himself" (Luke 24:27). Do you expect your students to think critically about what you teach and what God wants them to obey? Do you allow time for them to share their insights?

Jesus held the Word as true. Jesus didn't say that God's Word *contains* truth. Instead, the disciples heard Him pray, "Your word is truth" (John 17:17). Do you feel confident that you're boldly proclaiming the truth?

Jesus used the Scriptures as the basis of spiritual formation. When Jesus gave God's Word to the disciples, they took on the characteristics of the Lord. Jesus said, "I have given them your word and the world has hated them, for they are not of the world any more than I am of the world. My prayer is not that you take them out of the world but that you protect them from the evil one" (John 17:14-15). Do you consider the Bible to be your meditation, your guide and your delight? Or are you still content to live in the world?

Jesus relied on the Word to do God's will. Jesus helped His followers understand that knowing God's will comes from knowing God's Word. Referring to Psalm 40, Jesus said, "Here I am—it is written about me in the scroll—I have come to do your will, O God" (Heb. 10:7). Do you model to your students what it means to live within God's will based on the Scriptures, even when you don't know His will for a specific situation?

How Do We Teach the Scriptures?

If Jesus had such a fundamental view of Scripture, it makes sense that we should also study, practice and teach God's Word.

The Bible helps us tutor a student's search for truth. "For the word of God is living and active. Sharper than any double-edged sword, it penetrates even to dividing soul and spirit, joints and marrow; it judges the thoughts and attitudes of the heart" (Heb. 4:12). The Bible guides and shapes our students' search for the realities of life (see Deut. 30:11-16). The Bible gives us insight into studying the Word itself (see John 17:17). And the Bible tells us how to have a personal relationship with the Lord Jesus Christ (see John 5:39).

Yet so many people don't seem to live for Christ. Why? Perhaps they've only learned to know the Word, but not to obey the Word. I'm a good example of knowing Scripture but not obeying it. I grew up a "Bible brat." I memorized entire passages of the New Testament and even some from the Old Testament. I could tell you the longest chapter in the Bible, the shortest chapter, the shortest verse, the shortest verse in the Greek language, the verse in the middle of the Bible . . . and so on.

But who cares? Was any life change connected to this knowledge? Sure, my Sunday School teachers and Children's Church teachers taught me the truths of Christ. Youth leaders modeled the Christ life. My family trained me in the way of Christ. This was all valuable. But until I made a fullhearted commitment to live for Christ, my Bible knowledge wasn't all-authoritative for me.

Now, as I learn to obey—even well into adulthood—I realize what the psalmist meant when he proclaimed that God's Law, statutes, precepts, commands and ordinances "are more precious than gold, than much pure gold; they are sweeter than honey, than honey from the comb . . . in keeping them there is great reward"(Ps. 19:10-11).

That's why I get so concerned with Bible teaching that does not lead to obedience! As author and Bible teacher Bruce Wilkerson notes, "There is an indescribable difference between teaching the facts and teaching lives to change on the basis of the facts. Knowing the stories doesn't change anyone—just visit a secular college class on the 'Bible as Literature' and see for yourself."[1]

As teachers, sometimes we seem to be preparing our students to win at Bible trivia, but not to win at obeying the Lord! We spend time drilling the Word into our students but miss the impact of what Scripture can mean for them. They get facts, but receive little faith. They can win debates, but not make biblical decisions. They can attend good spiritual services, but have no real desire to serve the Lord.

Jesus' Example

So how can rock-solid teachers help? We can follow Jesus' example! He knew His students. He obviously knew Scripture. And He knew how to prompt His students toward obedience.

Jesus Knew His Learners

Jesus addressed four kinds of learners when He taught, and we can expect to find the same types of students when we teach Scripture:

Those who are mistaken. When our students don't know God's Word, they easily misunderstand what Scripture means. When Jesus spoke to the Sadducees, He said, "Are you not in error because you do not know the Scriptures or the power of God?" (Mark 12:24). The apostle Paul addressed how to teach this kind of mistaken student:

And the Lord's servant must not quarrel; instead, he must be kind to everyone, able to teach, not resentful. Those who oppose him he must gently instruct, in the hope that God will grant them repentance leading them to a knowledge of the truth (2 Tim. 2:24-26).

We can also run into students who know God's Word but refuse to obey it. Think of the group that Jesus confronted the most in His ministry—the Pharisees. These religious leaders knew all the ins and outs of the Scriptures but didn't allow any of its truths to affect them.

Those who are ignorant. As a Bible college professor for many years, I'm often surprised by people's ignorance about the stories and truths from Scripture. I'm even more surprised about the lack of concern over this shortage of knowledge. When we teach, we should follow the example of young Timothy's mother and grandmother, who trained him in the Scriptures:

But as for you, continue in what you have learned and have become convinced of, because you know those from whom you learned it, and how from infancy you have known the holy Scriptures, which are able to make you wise for salvation through faith in Christ Jesus. All Scripture is God-breathed and is useful for teaching, rebuking, correcting and training in righteousness, so that the man of God may be thoroughly equipped for every good work (2 Tim. 3:14-17).

God's Word was profitable in Timothy's life for salvation, edification and service.

Those who miss the power of Scripture. It's possible for our students to know much about the Bible yet not obey it because they don't understand the power of God's promises! As the apostle Peter assured his readers:

We did not follow cleverly invented stories when we told you about the power and coming of our Lord Jesus Christ, but we were eyewitnesses of his majesty. . . . And we have the word of the prophets made more certain, and you will do well to pay attention to it, as to a light shining in a dark place, until the day dawns and the morning star rises in your hearts (2 Pet. 1:16,19).

I remember counseling a man named Robert at the Omaha Open Door Mission. Robert responded after one of the first sermons I'd ever preached. We began talking about how Christ meets our need for a Savior. Before long, I realized that Robert knew more Scripture than I did! Obviously, somewhere along the line, Robert had missed the power of the Lord.

Those who gain insight into what to obey. These are students who understand the Word, apply the Word and obey the Word. After the resurrection, when Jesus' disciples suddenly understood that they had been conversing with the risen Lord, they said to each other, "Were not our hearts burning within us while he talked with us on the road and opened the Scriptures to us?" (Luke 24:32).

Jesus Knew Scripture

In addition to knowing His learners, Jesus also knew Scripture. Interestingly, sometimes knowing a biblical command can be aided by knowing what it isn't!

Knowing isn't a substitute for applying the Bible. If you know all the traffic laws and have memorized the driver's manual but you still speed, run red lights and drive in opposing traffic, you probably won't survive very long. You need to apply what you know when you get behind the wheel. The same is true of God's Word. Professor Howard Hendricks describes the religious leaders of Jesus' day who knew the Scripture but didn't apply it:

The classic illustration of interpretation without application is the scribes and Pharisees. These religionists had all of the data. They had mastered the Old Testament, but they were never mastered by the truth. Did they know where the Messiah was to be born? Absolutely. They were authorities on that: Bethlehem of Judea, of course. But when the report came, did they go down to check it out? No, even though the town was only five miles down the road. Unfortunately, their knowledge created no responsibility within them . . . Why not? Because all of their righteousness was external. It was based on facts. It never led to a personal response.[2]

I once heard a teacher lovingly tease his adult Sunday School class: "You people are educated way beyond your obedience. You know stuff you don't intend to obey!"

Busyness isn't a substitute for applying the Bible. Once again, the religious leaders of Jesus' day provide an example. While they busily followed details about tithing, they seemed unconcerned about bigger issues, such as showing justice and mercy to others. Jesus blasted them:

> Woe to you, teachers of the law and Pharisees, you hypocrites! You give a tenth of your spices—mint, dill and cummin. But you have neglected the more important matters of the law—justice, mercy and faithfulness. You should have practiced the latter, without neglecting the former (Matt. 23:23).

Superficial obedience isn't a substitute for applying the Bible. After Jesus miraculously fed the 5,000, most of the crowd continued to follow Him because of the bread they were fed. But Jesus challenged them to go deeper:

> "I tell you the truth, you are looking for me, not because you saw miraculous signs but because you ate the loaves and had your fill. Do not work for food that spoils, but for food that endures to eternal life, which the Son of Man will give you. On him God the Father has placed his seal of approval." Then they asked him, "What must we do to do the works God requires?" Jesus answered, "The work of God is this: to believe in the one he has sent" (John 6:26-29).

Jesus Knew How to Prompt Students to Obey

Jesus knew His students and the Scriptures. In addition, He knew how to teach so that His students would want to obey. Look at what occurred when Jesus taught:

- People were healed (see Matt. 4:23).
- Crowds were astonished at His authority (see Matt. 7:28-29; 22:33).
- Cities came to know His compassion (see Matt. 9:35-36).
- Disciples experienced heart-integration training (see Matt. 15:7-19).
- Enemies were confounded (see Matt. 21:23-27).
- Every person on Earth was targeted to be taught toward obedience (Matt. 28:18-20).

If Jesus taught in such a way that people applied what they learned, how should we be teaching?

Putting Jesus' Method of Teaching Scripture into Practice

Naturally, we should teach with the same commitment of knowing our students, knowing God's Word, and leading our students toward life change. Author Dave Veerman puts it this way: "Application focuses the truth of God's Word to specific, life-related situations. It helps people understand what to do or how to use what they have learned."[3]

So how can rock-solid teachers do this in practical ways?

With Children

- *Know your students.* What's clear to you from Scripture might not be easy for children to understand. Read and listen to others who work with the same age group. For example:
   - Talk to other teachers, fellow Sunday School and club leaders, and other instructors such as drama teachers, piano tutors and coaches.

▫ Read the curriculum you're using. Often, curriculum writers provide solid help for students at a particular age level that can help you in your own teaching.

▫ Read reliable materials from educators who know children. For example, the following excerpts from *How to Have a Great Sunday School: Sunday School Standards for All Age Groups* provide practical advice for making sure you know your students:

- *Physical:* Monitor the room's lighting, temperature and air flow to ensure student comfort.
- *Social:* Plan ways for your class to interact and work together.
- *Emotional:* Show respect and acceptance for a student who might be upset, bored or fearful.
- *Intellectual:* Allow students the freedom to disagree with you without rejecting them.
- *Spiritual:* Actively seek to discover each student's spiritual condition and attitudes.
- *Age Level:* Plan ways to accommodate different skill levels of students in your class.
- *Individual:* Use varied teaching approaches to accommodate the different learning styles of your students.[4]

- *Prompt life change.* Ask questions to prompt application. For example:

    ▫ What does that verse mean?
    ▫ Can you say this verse in your own words?
    ▫ Is there anything from this verse that you should obey this next week?
    ▫ How might you share this story with a friend or family member?
    ▫ Can you remember another verse or story that says the same thing?
    ▫ Have you seen anyone use this verse or principle?

With Youth

- *Know your content.* Memorize several of the following verses on application with the teenagers in your group:

  - Genesis 18:19
  - Psalm 119:9,11
  - Jeremiah 15:16
  - Matthew 5:16
  - Acts 17:11
  - Romans 15:4
  - 2 Timothy 3:14-17
  - James 4:17
  - Revelation 1:3

- *Prompt life change.* When the "What Would Jesus Do?" (WWJD) reminders were popular a few years ago, one of the guys in my youth group asked, "How can you choose to do what Jesus would do when you don't know what Jesus did?" Good question! Here are some ways you can help youth move toward application:

  - After studying a Bible passage, ask three questions:

    1. Is there anything I should stop doing?
    2. Is there anything I should start doing?
    3. Is there anything I should strengthen (continue) doing?

  - Create an O.A.T.S. sheet:
    - **O** = *Objective:* What would I like to see happen in my life?
    - **A** = *Activity:* What activities would create that life change?
    - **T** = *Timetable:* When and where will this happen?
    - **S** = *Systematic Checkup:* What systems of accountability do I need?

▫ Simply ask, "What's your plan?"

▫ Create a Hitting the Target application sheet:

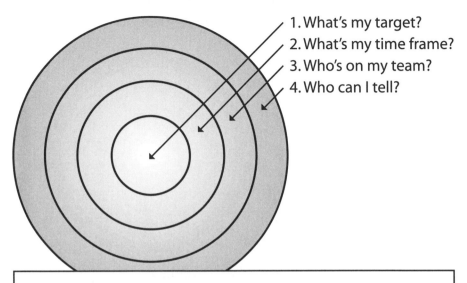

1. What's my target?
2. What's my time frame?
3. Who's on my team?
4. Who can I tell?

1. What's my target—what do I think God wants me to do?
2. What's my time frame—what's preventing me from doing this right now?
3. Who's on my team—who can help me with my decision?
4. Who can I tell—what one person can mentor me or partner with me in this?

With Adults

• *Know your content.* Missions leader and author Hans Finzel asks three important questions that can help teachers prepare their content for application:

  1. Is this teaching local or universal? Is this truth for a specific group at a specific location, or is it intended for everyone at all times?
  2. Is the teaching temporary or timeless? Is this truth to be applied in only a certain period of history, or is it always applicable?
  3. What realm of experience does this passage speak to? In what areas of our lives should we apply these truths?[5]

• *Prompt life change.* Use the following grid for application. I use it when I prepare lessons, and I occasionally train students to use it for their own growth and spiritual formation. Looking at the relationships of your life between God, yourself, others and the Enemy, the Holy Spirit can reveal blind spots and motivate you toward action steps of obedience.

Your Relationship to God	Your Relationship to Yourself	Your Relationship to Others	Your Relationship to the Enemy
Fellowship to Enjoy	Past Needing Healing	In Home	Temptations to Resist
Commands to Obey	Present Experience	In Church	Devices to Recognize
Promises to Claim	Personal Priorities and Values	In the Community	Snares to Avoid
Promises to Express	Future Expectations	In Society	Armor to Wear

With Your Own Family

• *Know your student and your content.* My family found these practical values emerge as we participated in an intergenerational experience called Family Together Sunday School:[6]

□ Time spent in play and conversation is valuable for biblical obedience. Parents were surprised to find they had deeper insight through this kind of activity.

□ Reading the Bible and responding to children's questions can help parents grasp the deeper meaning of verses they've known for years. The fresh insight of see-ing application through a child's eyes prompted the parents' faith.

▫ Motivation to build deeper relationships and deeper meaning of Scripture is greatly aided from routines that kids love. Children at the event would say things such as, "Mom, Dad, it's time to do our Bible reading!" This encouraged families to stay consistent.

▫ Teenagers tend to apply Scripture to their own lives when they learn it in a multigenerational context. Different viewpoints need to be implemented, or we can become very narrow in our peer culture or domi-nant age-grouped perspective.

• *Prompt application by referring back to Scripture.* One dad I know asks his children to recall what Bible verse might apply in spe-cific situations. This ties what children learn at church with their behavior at home: "These commandments that I give you today are to be upon your hearts. Impress them on your chil-dren. Talk about them when you sit at home and when you walk along the road, when you lie down and when you get up" (Deut. 6:6-7).

Self-Check

Before you turn to chapter 8, take a few minutes to evaluate how you're fulfilling your role as a rock-solid teacher in the area of knowing your students, knowing God's Word, and helping your students move toward life change. Just between you and God, rate how you're doing at teach-ing in these areas. Spend some time in prayer asking God to help you grow in areas in which you're struggling.

Know Your Students

I'm knowledgeable about my students. I've established relationships that allow me to shepherd them on a consistent basis.

strongly agree   *agree*   *not sure*   *disagree*   *strongly disagree*

I set aside time to engage in meaningful conversation and activity both in and outside of class.

strongly agree   *agree*   *not sure*   *disagree*   *strongly disagree*

I can name several of my students' friends and the impact they've had on the spiritual development of that individual.

strongly agree   *agree*   *not sure*   *disagree*   *strongly disagree*

Know the Content of Scripture

I'm aware of Scripture. I observe and interpret God's Word appropriately.

strongly agree   *agree*   *not sure*   *disagree*   *strongly disagree*

I memorize Scripture, believing the promise of Psalm 119:10-11: "I seek you with all my heart; do not let me stray from your commands. I have hidden your word in my heart that I might not sin against you."

strongly agree   *agree*   *not sure*   *disagree*   *strongly disagree*

I gather with believers of different ages and different life situations to learn the Scriptures together.

strongly agree   *agree*   *not sure*   *disagree*   *strongly disagree*

I occasionally go deeper to experience new depths of Bible study. For example, I sometimes read extended passages or a Bible commentary.

strongly agree   *agree*   *not sure*   *disagree*   *strongly disagree*

Prompt Application and Life Change

I prepare my own heart for application and expect the Holy Spirit to change me and help me grow. I know that I can't take others where I refuse to go.

strongly agree   *agree*   *not sure*   *disagree*   *strongly disagree*

I plan to lead students toward life change through using creative and specific methods that help them apply what they're learning.

strongly agree   *agree*   *not sure*   *disagree*   *strongly disagree*

I ask how my family or my students have applied the Scripture that they have studied.

strongly agree   *agree*   *not sure*   *disagree*   *strongly disagree*

Benediction

May the Lord Jesus Christ, who was and is the Word, fill you with the knowledge and application of His will, and may you know the joy of seeing your students incarnate the truth you teach and model. Amen.

CHAPTER 8

USE THINGS, NOT PEOPLE

Key Idea: Rock-solid teachers use the teaching environment to prepare students to learn.

*As he was leaving the temple, one of his disciples said to him,
"Look, Teacher! What massive stones! What magnificent buildings!"
"Do you see all these great buildings?" replied Jesus. "Not one stone here
will be left on another; every one will be thrown down." As Jesus was
sitting on the Mount of Olives opposite the temple, Peter, James, John
and Andrew asked him privately, "Tell us, when will these things happen?
And what will be the sign that they are all about to be fulfilled?"*

MARK 13:1-4

A few years ago, I helped Neil, a club leader, with his class. The situation was a bit unusual, because carpenters had been doing some remodeling in the room but hadn't finished their work. In addition to the power and hand tools they left behind—a major temptation for a group of third-grade boys—the workers had also left some good-sized messes. Sawdust covered parts of the carpet, wood scraps were scattered about the room, and other trash littered the classroom.

Neil—who was also a church trustee—decided to use the built-in labor and unending energy of his students to clean up what the carpenters had left behind. In the midst of putting his class to work picking up trash and vacuuming the new carpet, Neil spent considerable time issuing commands: "Don't touch those tools!" "Leave that stuff alone!" and "Stay away from that table saw!" It was a little much for me—even though I grew up wondering if my name was "Stop that, Greg!" The class never did get to their lesson. But they sure had a fine-looking classroom!

This teacher seemed to have the motto of using *students* to serve *things*.

Compare his perspective with this one: Not long ago, I met a youth leader, Beth, who somehow had talked the leaders of her church into building a skateboard ramp in the church parking lot. As a result, the kids who came to use the jumps on skates, rollerblades and BMX bikes—as well as the ones who came just to hang around—had trampled much of the lawn near the ramps. "When I compare the way our church looks to others around town, it looks bad!" Beth exclaimed. "Isn't that great?"

I wasn't quite expecting that last statement from Beth. She was excited about the extra wear and tear on the church property because she'd made a commitment that the church would be a place where youth-group teens could invite their friends to hang out. Not far from the ramps and trampled lawn stood a worn-out basketball hoop and some battered picnic tables and benches. Beth said that she'd had amazing conversations with teenagers from the community who vowed they'd never come inside the church doors.

This leader knew the secret of using *things* to serve *students*.

The first teacher emphasized taking care of the facilities that God provides. So far, nothing wrong with that. However, when we begin to think that material things are ends in themselves, we have a problem. On the other hand, some might accuse the second teacher of bad stewardship in not taking care of what God had provided. Many teachers know the frustration of having to clean up after another class, or doing without a computer because it just happened to be needed in another area, or being left with a broken chair because the youth group got a bit out of control.

How Did Jesus Find Balance?

The good news is that we can find a proper balance between practicing good stewardship and using things to serve students—and perhaps erring on the side of the latter. Jesus demonstrated this balance well in the ways He used the environment and settings of His teaching.

Environment Enhances Worship

One of Jesus' disciples commented on the beauty and the grandeur of Jerusalem's Temple. Yet Jesus said that it would be destroyed (see Mark 13:1-2). If you think about it, from where Jesus came in heaven, the stuff we count most precious—gold—is used for asphalt!

Isn't it ironic? The very building meant to help people worship God had become a place of marketing and covering of the meaning of true worship. Do you remember Jesus' words to the Samaritan woman when she confused the purpose of the *place* of worship?

> Jesus declared, "Believe me, woman, a time is coming when you will worship the Father neither on this mountain nor in Jerusalem. You Samaritans worship what you do not know; we worship what we do know, for salvation is from the Jews. Yet a time is coming and has now come when the true worshipers will worship the Father in spirit and truth, for they are the kind of worshipers the Father seeks" (John 4:21-23).

This serves as a potent reminder that the place we worship enhances our internal attitudes. Yet we shouldn't be so impressed by environmental factors that we miss the larger concept of worship from the heart. Consider the following ways that the learning environment can enhance this kind of worship for your students:

Deepen student responsiveness. Should we avoid using fine architecture and beautiful buildings to honor God? Of course not! The same Lord who cleansed the Temple also commissioned Solomon to build the first one as a glorious and holy place: "I intend, therefore, to build a temple for the Name of the LORD my God, as the LORD told my father David, when he said, 'Your son whom I will put on the throne in your place will build the temple for my Name'" (1 Kings 5:5).

The same Lord who predicted the demise of the Temple also gave orders for building a beautiful tabernacle. The Lord told Moses: "Then have them make a sanctuary for me, and I will dwell among them. Make this tabernacle and all its furnishings exactly like the pattern I will show you" (Exod. 25:8-9).

If we want to help our students connect with God, it's important that we make sure they're not distracted from meeting Him. In addition, we can provide a setting where we help people understand the symbols and actions we use in worship. And we can approach learning and worship times with creativity and variety.

Urge students toward awe. While the moneychangers were eager for gain, Jesus knew the value of a place by the function it fulfilled, not by its business. He said, "My house will be a house of prayer" (Luke 19:46). In your teaching setting, this might mean being less concerned about keeping a tight schedule and maintaining strict discipline and more concerned about setting aside time for Bible reading, prayer and good conversation centered on the Lord.

Cause students to ponder. In Mark 5:24-32, when crowds gathered because they wanted to hear Jesus, He was concerned with one individual in the crowd who touched Him. Think of all the questions this one incident raises:

- Why was Jesus caught in this crush of people?
- How did Jesus know this one woman touched Him, when He was jostled by many in the crowd?

- Why did the disciples react the way they did?
- How did Jesus respond to this interruption?
- How do we respond to interruptions?
- Did Jesus already know the answer when He asked, "Who touched my clothes?" (v. 30).
- Why did Jesus call the woman out of the crowd?
- What did He say to her, and why?

Notice that this scene took place far from the Temple or any other formal place of worship. Yet it was environment that provided many ways for students to ponder and grow in their faith.

Prompt students to faith. When the crowds followed Jesus because He had provided food, Jesus reminded them: "Do not work for food that spoils, but for food that endures to eternal life" (John 6:27).

What an interesting set of circumstances. A crowd followed Jesus because He fed them, and He used the setting and the very thing the people wanted—food—to teach them about faith.

When you teach, what circumstances, objects and settings can you use to prompt your students to increase their faith?

Drive students to service. Jesus saw environment as useful when it assisted people in worshiping the living God through their service. After He spoke to the Samaritan woman at the well, she understood and accepted that Jesus was the promised Messiah. And she immediately began to serve Him—even leaving the precious water jars she'd brought to the well. She went into the city and promptly started to tell other people about Jesus (John 4:28-29).

Environment Enhances Learning

The learning environment should also help our students focus on knowing, loving and learning about God. When Jesus taught, He regularly used simple illustrations and the natural environment to help people grasp spiritual truths.

Simple illustrations. Look at some of the illustrations Jesus used from everyday life to portray deep spiritual concepts:

- Soils showed how Christians respond to God's Word (see Luke 8:5-15).
- A child demonstrated humility and greatness in the kingdom of God (see Matt. 18:2-4).
- A lily was used to show how we shouldn't worry (Matt. 6:28).
- An ox in a well was used to rebuke hypocrisy (see Luke 14:1-6).
- A handful of grain served as a spiritual heart check (see John 12:23-28).
- A rock-solid house provided a lesson in obedience (see Matt. 7:24-27).
- A boy's lunch became an investment in faith (see John 6:1-9).
- A coin demonstrated paying honor where it's due (see Matt. 22:19-21).
- A towel became an example of servant leadership (see John 13:4-15).
- A piece of bread and a cup of wine provided a call to remembrance (see Luke 22:17-20).
- A cross became a symbol of reconciliation (see Col. 1:19-23).
- An empty tomb provided evidence of new birth (see 1 Pet. 1:3).

Think about the everyday objects you can incorporate into your teaching. For example, I remember participating in a Bible lesson that used objects already present in the room. I went first, and my object was a Styrofoam cup.

Here's what I came up with: "When I drink from a cup, I think of being thirsty. Jesus said, 'Will you give me a drink?' in John 4:7. I also think of rivers of living water (see John 7:38). If we believe, the Holy Spirit will be like 'streams of living water.' The cup is plain. I think of how God's surpassing glory is displayed through us earthen vessels (see 2 Cor. 4:7). Finally, I don't want to be like the Pharisees, who washed the outside of the cup but inside were full of greed and sin (see Matt. 23:25-27)."

Natural surroundings. Jesus fit His teaching into His surroundings to prepare His students for learning. Consider the variety of places where Jesus taught:

- By the Jordan River (see Mark 1:9)
- In the wilderness (see Mark 1:12-13)
- Beside the Sea of Galilee (see Mark 1:16; 4:1)
- In the synagogue (see Mark 1:21)
- At the house of Simon (see Mark 1:29-34)
- In a solitary place (see Mark 1:35)
- At a home with a hole in the roof (see Mark 2:1-12)
- Reclining at table (see Mark 2:15-17)
- In the grain fields (Mark 2:23-28)
- In a boat on the Sea of Galilee (see Mark 3:9-12)
- On the mountain (see Mark 3:13)
- In a foreign country—the region of Gerasenes (see Mark 5:1)
- Along the road (see Mark 5:31-35)
- In the synagogue ruler's house (see Mark 5:36-43)
- In His hometown (see Mark 6:1)
- In a deserted place (see Mark 6:31-32)
- Walking on the Sea of Galilee (see Mark 6:45-52)
- In villages, cities and countrysides (see Mark 6:56)
- In a marketplace or field (see Mark 7:1-7)
- In a house away from the crowd (see Mark 7:17)
- In Tyre, Sidon, Decapolis and the Dalmanutha regions (see Mark 7:24—8:10)
- In villages in Caesarea Philippi (see Mark 8:27)

And that's just from the first eight chapters of Mark! Now, notice the times Jesus taught:

- On a work day (see Mark 1:16-18)
- On the Sabbath (see Mark 1:21)
- In the evening (see Mark 1:32)
- In the early morning, while it was still dark—right after the evening teaching and healing the night before! (see Mark 1:35-37)
- During extended teaching tours (see Mark 1:39)
- At home during lunchtime and dinnertime (see Mark 3:20)
- During travel times, solitary times and regular times (see Mark 5:1; 6:32; 6:53-56)

- From noon until three in the afternoon, on the cross (see Mark 15:33-34)
- Very early on the first day of the week (see Mark 16:2)

Again, these are from just a short survey of Mark's Gospel.

Jesus taught in a variety of places and at all times of the day and night. Most of the places He taught were not like classrooms at all. Perhaps as much as 80 percent of Jesus' teaching took place in unconventional locations or informal settings.

When you consider all the places and times where and when Jesus taught, be open and willing to teach using the following principles:

- *Take advantage of the teaching settings before you.* Look for ways to bring the teaching of God's Word into everyday life. For example, use singing and other music to teach, carry verse cards or gospel tracts to share, or equip students with skills and tools to witness.

- *Make your classroom setting more inviting.* Use real-life examples and activities as opportunities for informality in your learning times.

- *Seek to be in control of the learning environment.* Pick up clutter and clean rooms and furniture. Paint a dull room, or hang photos or a mural to enhance a room.

- *Don't confine your instructional ministry to a classroom.* Teach in the car, at home, around a table, in the church parking lot, in the hallway, and in other informal settings.

A friend of mine who grew up in a small rural church vividly remembers going to his junior high Sunday School class in the kitchen basement of the church! He recalls that his creative teacher made it seem completely natural—and even special—to discuss spiritual matters next to everyday objects like the kitchen sink and refrigerator while the potluck food stayed warm in the oven.

Environment Enhances Fellowship

Near the end of His earthly ministry, Jesus shared the Passover meal that we call the Last Supper with His apostles:

> So he sent two of his disciples, telling them, "Go into the city, and a man carrying a jar of water will meet you. Follow him. Say to the owner of the house he enters, 'The Teacher asks: Where is my guest room, where I may eat the Passover with my disciples?' He will show you a large upper room, furnished and ready. Make preparations for us there" (Mark 14:13-15).

Notice the intensity and urgency in Jesus' remarks during the meal: "When the hour came, Jesus and his apostles reclined at the table. And he said to them, 'I have eagerly desired to eat this Passover with you before I suffer'" (Luke 22:14-15).

Jesus was very aware of how the setting—the last occasion before He would become the perfect Passover sacrifice—would enhance fellowship with those closest to Him.

Environment Enhances Service

When Jesus chose His apostles, He commissioned them with the idea of preparing them to serve: "He appointed twelve—designating them apostles—that they might be with him and that he might send them out to preach" (Mark 3:14).

With the Twelve, Jesus used a variety of settings to accomplish deeper discipleship and stronger service, and to launch new leaders. Essentially, Jesus did a lot of on-the-job training.

As you teach your students, remember this basic principle of service: We need to spend time with Jesus before we can serve as His representatives.

Putting Jesus' Method of Using the Environment into Practice

As rock-solid teachers, we can imitate Jesus' practice of using the learning environment to enhance worship, learning, fellowship and service.

Here are some specific ideas:

With Children

- *Teach stillness and reverence.* Occasionally speak with the children in hushed tones, using "our inside voices."

- *Keep classrooms clean and safe.*

- *Use simple illustrations and watch for too much symbolism.* Children tend to be concrete thinkers. However, capitalize on "show and tell" enthusiasm and be willing to use items that students bring to the classroom.

- *Teach Scripture truths during formal and informal times.* Students often learn as much during games or crafts as they do during lessons or story times. Learning about how to obey Jesus might occur on the gym floor more easily than it does during a small-group discussion.

- *Use guided conversation.* This way of directing thoughts in natural conversation follows the advice of Deuteronomy 6:7: "You shall teach them diligently to your children, and shall talk of them when you sit in your house, when you walk by the way, when you lie down, and when you rise up" (*NKJV*). (For a more complete description of guided conversation, see chapter 6, "Putting Jesus' Method of Motivating Students into Practice.")

- *Encourage students to serve with the natural enthusiasm they already possess.* Allow children to assist in classroom preparation as the class proceeds. They'll accomplish a lot, and you'll be preparing future ministry leaders.

- *Establish the best places and ways for learning to take place.* Tools such as *Gospel Light's Children's Ministry Smart Pages*[1] can help you evaluate:

□ How to organize for learning

□ What equipment should be in a classroom

□ The layout of the room for providing maximum learning

□ Safety and health procedures and policies

□ What to include in a resource room[2]

□ How to decorate your classroom

• *Establish standards for learning.* Among my favorite resources is *How to Have a Great Sunday School: Sunday School Standards for All Age Groups.*[3]

With Youth

• *Use music to enhance your message.* Make sure the music doesn't cover what you're trying to communicate. Aim for not too boring, not too radical. Know your audience.

• *Stock your classroom with interesting objects, pictures and teaching materials.* You never know when a map, an illustrative object or a prop will deepen your instruction.

    When I spoke to a youth group about a mission trip to Russia, I brought a set of those wooden stacking dolls. However, these dolls weren't the traditional ones with colorful cultural dress. They were of the Dream Team. It drove home the point that most Russian teenagers know more about basketball teams than they do about the heroes of the Bible—not unlike American teens.

• *Get to know your site and adjust it to serve your needs of teaching.* Use a Site Inspection chart like the one found in *Youth Ministry Management Tools*[4] to evaluate items such as accessibility, safety, facility flexibility, usability and prices.

• *Spend time with the teens in your group.* Follow the practical and effective principle, "Take them with you where you are. Go with them where they are!"

- *Provide on-the-job training to help teenagers feel valued.* Encourage teens to lead Bible studies, host prayer groups, and serve in other creative venues.

- *Walk through your learning areas with a visitor's eyes.* Walls that need to be cleaned or painted, floors that need attention, and other visual clutter can distract from learning. Informality doesn't have to equal messy.

With Adults

- *Use word pictures when teaching adults.* Using metaphors, memory devices and object lessons isn't just for kids.

- *Encourage adult students to get involved in repairing and creating the learning environment for the entire church.* Coordinate work days to clean your church facilities or adopt a children's Sunday School classroom that the adult students can decorate and organize.

- *View the classroom as a training facility for deployment of a skilled worker into the Kingdom harvest work.* The more you can get adult students to practice a skill in the learning setting, the more effective the training will be.

- *Do a lighting and visibility check.* Ask your students if they can see you. Some senior adults, for example, read lips to enhance what they hear. Make sure you allow for every learner to be able to see what's going on. And teach yourself to speak to your students rather than the whiteboard!

- *Encourage adults to use verse-card sets and other mnemonic devices to memorize Scripture.* One helpful tool is *The Topical Bible Memory System* from the Navigators.[5]

With Your Own Family

- *Evaluate rooms in your home for their learning potential.* For example, if you own a TV set, is it the focal point of the room? Why? In fact, you might want to consider participating in the Great American TV Off week. "Unplug the drug!" Connect the event to spiritual teachings by placing the following verses on the TV screen as a reminder to leave the set off:

> Finally, brothers, whatever is true, whatever is noble, whatever is right, whatever is pure, whatever is lovely, whatever is admirable—if anything is excellent or praiseworthy—think about such things (Phil. 4:8).

> I will set before my eyes no vile thing (Ps. 101:3).

Remind family members to *not* watch TV for an entire week. Use the extra time to play with your kids, have conversations, read and participate in activities together as a family.

- *Provide objects that can enhance the spiritual growth of your children.* When our sons were young, we purchased an inexpensive nativity set that they could play with rather than just look at. We were surprised how they told the story of Christ's birth again and again.

- *Provide reminders of spiritual principles in your home.* "These commandments that I give you today are to be upon your hearts . . . Write them on the doorframes of your houses and on your gates" (Deut. 6:6,9). Some ideas:

  □ Post a spiritual growth chart. Mark not only the height of the kids, but also significant spiritual events that occur in their lives.

- Take an inventory of what hangs on the walls of your children's rooms. Do any photos or posters contradict or ridicule Jesus? Are any Scripture passages or stories portrayed?
- Place missionary prayer cards on your refrigerator. Urge your children to pray for those missionaries when they reach inside for a snack.

• *Think about what the exterior of your home communicates.* Some ideas:

- Cut your lawn and maintain the exterior of your home as a good testimony to your neighbors. Assist your neighbors with cleaning, raking, shoveling snow and other simple outdoor tasks.
- Use Christian symbols when you decorate for Christmas and other holidays.
- Make your home a "safe house" in which kids and parents know they're welcome if anyone is in need.
- Invite your neighbors to read through the Bible with you this year. Provide copies of a reading plan, such as the one offered by Discipleship Journal.[6]

Self-Check

Before you turn to chapter 9, take a few minutes to evaluate how you're fulfilling your role as a rock-solid teacher in the area of using environment to help students learn. Just between you and God, rate how you're doing at teaching in this area. Spend some time in prayer asking God to help you grow in areas in which you're struggling.

Enhancing Worship
I set up my classroom so that students respond to the Lord. I minimize distractions, interruptions and messy or unclean surroundings.

strongly agree   *agree*   *not sure*   *disagree*   *strongly disagree*

I use posters, bulletin boards, and other materials in the classroom to inspire reverence and thought.

strongly agree   *agree*   *not sure*   *disagree*   *strongly disagree*

I record experiences in a class journal or in drawings of what God has done with the students: Answers to prayer, times of revival, memories of worship times, and so forth.

strongly agree   *agree*   *not sure*   *disagree*   *strongly disagree*

Enhancing Learning

I use the environment to enhance learning through a healing climate, available resources and appropriate preparation.

strongly agree   *agree*   *not sure*   *disagree*   *strongly disagree*

I bring informality into learning times by using real-life examples and activities.

strongly agree   *agree*   *not sure*   *disagree*   *strongly disagree*

Variety in schedule and availability are a part of my teaching.

strongly agree   *agree*   *not sure*   *disagree*   *strongly disagree*

Enhancing Fellowship

I use the learning environment to enhance fellowship by making our classroom settings inviting.

strongly agree   *agree*   *not sure*   *disagree*   *strongly disagree*

I make sure that temperature, lighting and seating are comfortable and appropriate.

strongly agree   *agree*   *not sure*   *disagree*   *strongly disagree*

I sometimes provide refreshments to encourage fellowship in the group.

strongly agree   *agree*   *not sure*   *disagree*   *strongly disagree*

Enhancing Service

I work with others in our church to make sure we provide opportunities

for service by not being too stiff and rigid about our buildings.
strongly agree   *agree*   *not sure*   *disagree*   *strongly disagree*

I provide places and times to pray for those who serve our church, for missionaries, and for other Christian workers sent out from our church.
strongly agree   *agree*   *not sure*   *disagree*   *strongly disagree*

I occasionally plan a class or family project to work on together: putting together holiday food baskets, cleaning houses or raking yards, making Angel Tree projects for prisoners, doing special visitations for those who are sick, participating in evangelism events.
strongly agree   *agree*   *not sure*   *disagree*   *strongly disagree*

Benediction
May the Lord Jesus, who used all sorts of places to accomplish His will, feel at home in your heart through faith. Amen.

CHAPTER 9

KEEP THE MAIN THING THE MAIN THING

Key Idea: Rock-solid teachers shape lives to be like Christ.

Now this is eternal life: that they may know you, the only true God, and Jesus Christ, whom you have sent. I have brought you glory on earth by completing the work you gave me to do.

JOHN 17:3-4

Georgeʼs job during the midweek club ministry included checking in the children. He came up with a plan to do his job with flair—almost! But as he tried to implement his new system for the process, kids were left standing around the table, and parents became impatient. A number of them got tired of waiting and left with their kids.

Finally, George told teachers and other leaders to just take down the important information and move into the activities. Georgeʼs new process ended up shortening the game time. And because George was still working on the lists during the large-group time, the leaders couldnʼt get the kids organized into small groups, so they had to skip that time completely.

What happened? Because of many good things, the main things were missed.

Letʼs go a step further. Reggie McNeal, the leadership development director for the South Carolina Baptist Convention, says, "In my observation, most church leaders are preoccupied with the wrong questions. If you solve the wrong problems precisely, what have you accomplished? You have wasted a lot of energy and perhaps fooled yourself that you have done something significant."[1]

In other words, teachers must keep the main thing the main thing!

Why do we teach? To build the next generation? Because itʼs a great way to learn? Because we love the process? Because of the content? Because of the students? Those motivations are all fine, but *the reason we teach is to keep the main thing the main thing!*

What *is* the main thing? The primary purpose of our teaching is to bring glory to God. We teach so that everyone might know God through Jesus Christ, and by that bring Him glory.

The apostle Paul stated that everything that he taught was to shape people to be more like Jesus Christ: "We proclaim him, admonishing and teaching everyone with all wisdom, so that we may present everyone perfect in Christ. To this end I labor, struggling with all his energy, which so powerfully works in me" (Col. 1:28-29).

Why do we teach? We teach to bring God glory!

How Did Jesus Bring God Glory?

To understand how Jesus brought God glory and how we can bring God glory, we need to understand what glory is. Simply put, glory is the unveiling of God's character.

I like the way that some of the teenagers from a youth group I led described it. After one of our teaching times, they started to say to each other, "Excuse me, I believe I see Jesus in you!" Then they would describe how they'd observed the character of Christ reflected in the other person.

Keeping the main thing the main thing—bringing glory to God—means revealing Him to those around us. Glory means pointing others toward God. It means highlighting Him in everything we think, say and do. Once again, Jesus demonstrated how we can bring glory to God. Let's explore some of the ways Jesus brought glory to the Father.

Jesus Is the Revelation of God's Glory

Before Christ came into the world, He dwelt with the Father in heaven. Jesus prayed, "Father, glorify me in your presence with the glory I had with you before the world began" (John 17:5). When Jesus took on human form and entered the world, Scripture proclaims, "The Word became flesh and made his dwelling among us. We have seen his glory, the glory of the One and Only, who came from the Father, full of grace and truth" (John 1:14).

Years later, the apostle Peter affirmed that he'd been an eyewitness of Jesus' glory brought to light on the Mount of Transfiguration:

> We did not follow cleverly invented stories when we told you about the power and coming of our Lord Jesus Christ, but we were eyewitnesses of his majesty. For he received honor and glory from God the Father when the voice came to him from the Majestic Glory, saying, "This is my Son, whom I love; with him I am well pleased." We ourselves heard this voice that came from heaven when we were with him on the sacred mountain (2 Pet. 1:16-18).

The glory that Jesus displayed during His earthly ministry brought His disciples to faith: "This beginning of miracles did Jesus in Cana of Galilee, and manifested forth his glory; and his disciples believed on him" (John 2:11, *KJV*). The glory of Jesus rising from the dead declared Him "to be the Son of God with power, according to the spirit of holiness" (Rom. 1:4, *KJV*). And God's glory is fully represented in Jesus' character: "The Son is the radiance of God's glory and the exact representation of his being, sustaining all things by his powerful word" (Heb. 1:3).

The glory Jesus shows will characterize His return. He won't come back as a carpenter, but as God! "For the Son of Man is going to come in his Father's glory with his angels, and then he will reward each person according to what he has done" (Matt. 16:27). When Jesus returns, all will acknowledge that He is God. Every eye will see, and every knee will bow (see Phil. 2:10).

Jesus always brought His Father glory. Jesus said to His disciples: "And I will do whatever you ask in my name, so that the Son may bring glory to the Father" (John 14:13). And Jesus' prayer in John 17 provides a glimpse of the glory of the Trinity. Jesus, God the Son, prays by the power of God the Holy Spirit to God the Father. And we get to listen in!

As teachers, we keep the main thing the main thing by revealing God's glory to our students.

Jesus Is the Reflection of God's Glory

In the Old Testament, God called on the nation of Israel to reflect His glory. In Isaiah's prophecy, for example, God said, "You are my servant, Israel, in whom I will display my splendor" (Isa. 49:3).

When Jesus was born, He became the perfect reflection of that glory. As Simeon blessed the baby Jesus, he said, "Sovereign Lord, as you have promised, you now dismiss your servant in peace. For my eyes have seen your salvation, which you have prepared in the sight of all people, a light for revelation to the Gentiles and for glory to your people Israel" (Luke 2:29-32).

Jesus reflected God's glory when He healed the blind man (see John 9:3) and when He raised Lazarus from the dead (see John 11:4). Most of all, Jesus reflected His Father's glory when He provided our means of salvation. The apostle Paul wrote, "The god of this age has blinded the minds of unbelievers, so that they cannot see the light of the gospel of the glory of Christ, who is the image of God" (2 Cor. 4:4).

Just as Jesus reflected God's character, His people should also reflect God's character. Our lives should reflect God's glory, and everything we do should be done for His glory. Paul wrote, "So whether you eat or drink or whatever you do, do it all for the glory of God" (1 Cor. 10:31). And Jesus Himself said, "Let your light so shine before men, that they may see your good works and glorify your Father in heaven" (Matt. 5:16, *NKJV*).

As teachers, we keep the main thing the main thing when we reflect God's glory to our students.

Jesus Is the Resource for God's Glory

If God wants us to show His character through our lives, what's the resource for our mission? The answer lies in the gifts that God gives us through the Holy Spirit. Before His crucifixion, Jesus retreated to pray for Himself, His disciples and all believers (see John 17). In this prayer, God provided the following resources for showing His glory:

When we lack confidence, the Lord gives authority. As Jesus prayed for Himself, He said, "For you granted him authority over all people that he might give eternal life to all those you have given him" (John 17:2). Just as the Father gave Jesus all authority (see Matt. 28:18), Jesus now sends us out to do His ministry with that same authority. Paul summarized it this way: "We are therefore Christ's ambassadors, as though God were making his appeal through us. We implore you on Christ's behalf: Be reconciled to God" (2 Cor. 5:20).

We can claim Jesus' authority to be confident in our teaching.

When we lack direction, the Lord gives work. Still praying for Himself in the hours before His impending arrest and crucifixion, Jesus prayed these astounding words to the Father: "I have brought you glory on earth by completing the work you gave me to do" (John 17:4). I find this prayer interesting because there were certainly more places for Jesus to preach the gospel, more interactions for Him to have with His disciples, and more people for Him to heal.

But Jesus had a sense of priority and purpose. When He healed a man who had been born blind, Jesus said, "As long as it is day, we must do the work of him who sent me. Night is coming, when no one can work. While I am in the world, I am the light of the world" (John 9:4-5). Earlier, He made clear that He was sent from the Father for a specific purpose: "For the very work that the Father has given me to finish, and which I am doing, testifies that the Father has sent me" (John 5:36). Jesus knew what to do because He knew who He was.

We derive our direction in teaching from the work given to Jesus.

When we lack motivation, the Lord gives glory. In John 17, Jesus prays for God's glory—the manifestation of God's character—to be a together experience: "glorify Me together with Yourself" (John 17:5, *NASB*). Jesus also prayed that God would give His glory to His disciples and followers:

> I have given them the glory that you gave me, that they may be one as we are one . . . Father, I want those you have given me to be with me where I am, and to see my glory, the glory you have given me because you loved me before the creation of the world (John 17:22,24).

God's glory provides the resources we need for almost any situation in life—even those that paralyze us from moving forward. If we're lonely, we can remember that God shares His glory through Christ. If we're afraid, the Lord draws us into oneness with Himself. If we're confused, the Lord guides us to new vistas of His glory. If we're in need, all of God's character is at hand in the glory of His grace:

> In him we have redemption through his blood, the forgiveness of sins, in accordance with the riches of God's grace that he lavished on us with all wisdom and understanding . . . in order that we, who were the first to hope in Christ, might be for the praise of his glory (Eph. 1:7-8,12).

We can find our sense of meaningfulness, oneness and purpose in the glory given to Jesus.

When we lack knowledge and wisdom, the Lord gives words. In John 17, when Jesus prayed for the disciples, He reminded the Father that the disciples had accepted Jesus' teaching and His identity as God:

> For I gave them the words you gave me and they accepted them. They knew with certainty that I came from you, and they believed that you sent me . . . I have given them your word and the world has hated them, for they are not of the world any more than I am of the world (John 17:8,14).

Notice the differing responses to Jesus: The disciples accepted the words and identity of the Lord, but the world hated the disciples and the Word that they believed.

I remember a time—shortly after the scandals involving a couple of televangelists—when I spoke to a local high school psychology class. The teacher wanted to engage me in a discussion on the hypocrisy of religion. When I asked God for wisdom, I felt led to stick closely with the topics that I'd been given and not to be lured into the teacher's debate. After the class, a number of the students asked if I could talk to them more about the nature of people, learning styles, how religion influences behavior and shapes our work ethic, and so forth. In other words, because I sensed and followed God's wisdom, students in the class learned from the topics I was prepared to speak on.

God can provide knowledge—His Word is truth (see John 17:17). Our Father gives wisdom—His Word is the basis of learning to fear Him. The apostle James put it in practical terms: "If any of you lacks wisdom, he should ask God, who gives generously to all without finding fault, and it will be given to him" (Jas. 1:5).

God's Word reveals His glory. We find the wisdom and knowledge we need in the words of our Lord.

When we lack identity, the Lord gives a name. Certain of His place in this world, Jesus said, "I will remain in the world no longer, but they are still in the world, and I am coming to you. Holy Father, protect them by the power of your name—the name you gave me—so that they may be one as we are one" (John 17:11).

God assists people in remembering the Name they have been called by: Jesus, a name above all others (see Phil. 2:9). God wants to protect us in the name of the Lord, and He wants us to be identified by our Christian character. Just as the Father and Son are united, God wants all believers to be united by being like the Lord Jesus.

Names provide definition, identity, a sense of belonging, meaning and protection. As two lines from a Tommy Walker song sung by our church's children's choir state, "He knows my name; He knows my every thought."[2] The clarification of who we are and what we're doing here comes from the name of Jesus given by the Father. What a comforting, motivating and encouraging idea.

We find the identity and protection we need in the glorious name of our Lord.

When we lack courage and hope, the Lord always gives love. Can we speak too much of Jesus' love? No! Jesus demonstrated His Father's love in tangible ways. In fact, probably the most well-known verse in the world shows just how much God loves us: "For God so loved the world that He gave His only begotten Son, that whoever believes in Him should not perish but have everlasting life" (John 3:16, *NKJV*).

In His prayer in John 17, Jesus asks the Father to continue to make known to His followers the great love the Father has for the Son: "I have made you known to them, and will continue to make you known in order that the love you have for me may be in them and that I myself may be in them" (v. 26).

The apostle Paul concluded that with God's great love as our resource, nothing can stop us from reflecting God's glory:

What, then, shall we say in response to this? If God is for us, who can be against us? He who did not spare his own Son, but gave him up for us all—how will he not also, along with him, graciously give us all things? Who will bring any charge against those whom God has chosen? It is God who justifies. Who is he that condemns? Christ Jesus, who died—more than that, who was raised to life—is at the right hand of God and is also interceding for us. Who shall separate us from the love of Christ? (Rom. 8:31-35).

We find all the courage and hope we need in the glorious love of Christ.

The prayer of our Savior in John 17 demonstrates that God has already provided the resources we need to teach effectively. As participants in these great glories, our teaching can be filled with joy and grace. As teachers, we keep the main thing the main thing by basing our teaching on the resources of the glory given to Jesus.

Jesus Is the Relationship of God's Glory

Jesus' extended prayer in John 17 also shows how a commitment to God's glory results in establishing three rock-solid relationships:

1. A relationship with the Father (see John 17:1-5)
2. A relationship with believers (see John 17:6-19)
3. A relationship with others so they may know Christ (see John 17:20-26)

Jesus modeled a relationship with the Father. When the religious leaders questioned the validity of Jesus' identity, He said, "And He who sent Me is with Me; He has not left Me alone, for I always do the things that are pleasing to Him" (John 8:29, *NASB*).

Jesus' relationship to the Father was the highest priority in His life. He really did fulfill the command: "Love the Lord your God with all your heart and with all your soul and with all your mind and with all your strength" (Mark 12:30).

Jesus modeled a relationship with those who believe. Referring to Jesus' humble act of washing the disciples' feet, John summarized this relationship in his Gospel: "Having loved His own who were in the world, He loved them to the end" (John 13:1, *NKJV*). This is the report of the loved disciple.

Because Jesus loved the disciples, He prayed for them to experience an overflowing relationship with the Father. He intends the same for us as His disciples today. Look at what Jesus prays for His followers:

• "That they may know you, the only true God, and Jesus Christ, whom you have sent" (John 17:3).

- "I have revealed you . . . and they have obeyed your word" (v. 6).
- "I gave them the words you gave me and they accepted them" (v. 8).
- "I pray for them . . . that they may be one" (vv. 9,11).
- "I protected them and kept them safe" (v. 12).
- "I say these things . . . so that they may have the full measure of my joy" (v. 13).
- "I have sent them" (v. 18).

Jesus modeled a relationship with those who didn't know Him. Jesus said, "My prayer is not for them alone. I pray also for those who will believe in me through their message" (John 17:20). We should note that the best ways for unbelievers to come to know Christ is by observing the oneness exhibited among those who already believe. Jesus prayed, "May they be brought to complete unity to let the world know that you sent me and have loved them even as you have loved me" (v. 23).

I remember one high school student, Wes, who honestly admitted, "I don't think I can handle becoming a Christian. It seems to me that those who talk the loudest about knowing God are the ones I hate to be around."

I assured him that I understood, and I even agreed that there seems to be enough hypocrisy around that all of us could have our fill. But I also reminded Wes of the faithfulness of the friend who invited him to youth group and the care the group demonstrated when they prayed for him. I added, "Jesus wants an intense and personal relationship with you! It would be a shame if others kept you away from that!"

On the way home that night, I gave thanks for a group of high school students who were living out the love of Christ for each other and who were modeling how the Lord Jesus wanted to reach those who didn't yet believe.

As teachers, we keep the main thing the main thing by keeping our relationships a top priority, following the Lord's example, and demonstrating the glory of Christ.

Putting Jesus' Method of Revealing God's Glory into Practice

One of the best ways to keep the main thing the main thing—revealing God's glory through Christ—involves maintaining a rich and vigorous prayer life. How can we accomplish the Lord's purposes and reveal His glory through prayer?

With Children

- *Remember important prayer requests.* Keep a record of your students' prayer requests in a prayer journal. This prompts faith, fellowship and relationships.

- *Plan unhurried times when you can pray with children.* Children's ministry experts Wes and Sheryl Haystead offer the following advice for helping kids pray:

  - Give children repeated opportunities to hear adults pray.
  - Keep your own prayers short. Avoid symbolism and flowery expressions.
  - Express your own feelings in prayer with children.[3]

The Haysteads conclude:

> When we spend time each day talking with God, when we turn first to Him in an anxious moment, when our thinking and our plans reflect our dependence upon His guidance, then children will sense through our attitudes and actions the reality of prayer in our own lives. Our task is to earnestly share with the children our deep belief in prayer. The result of our work is in the hands of the Holy Spirit.[4]

With Youth

- *Build relationships of healing by praying with teenagers.* Consider these intentional efforts in prayer:

  - Use 3" x 5" index cards or some other method to record prayer requests for the teenagers in your group. Update the records on a regular basis as students share new requests or report answers to prayer.
  - Ask teenagers to take the lead in building a prayer ministry in your youth ministry. Having students lead others in prayer ministry serves as a training ground to build faith and leadership.
  - Encourage prayer for the students. Ask parents to pray, prompt the church to pray, and make sure your church's prayer team remembers the youth ministry. Make it an all-out effort.

With Adults

- *Spend a half day or a full day with your adult group or class in prayer.* Plan to keep it simple:

  - Meet for orientation and preparation for a prolonged time of prayer. (Some groups like to prepare for the day ahead of time.)
  - Spend an extended time in personal prayer with your Bible, pen and notebook in hand.
  - Meet to discuss what you've learned that day.

- Some adult ministry guidelines in relation to prayer include:

  - Model prayer in and outside of class.
  - Don't assume that adults know how to pray. Teach specifics on the various kinds of prayer: conversational

prayer, prayers of praise, thanksgiving, confession, intercession, petition, outreach and a personal prayer life.
□ Create a prayer ministry in your church, or strengthen the intercessors groups that are already meeting.

With Your Family

- *Remind your family about the importance of prayer.* Subscribe to magazines and have books available to prompt prayer. I especially like *PrayKids!* published by the Navigators.[5] Another fine resource is *Let the Children Pray* by Esther Ilnisky, the founder of the Esther Network International Children's Global Prayer Movement.[6]

- *Establish specific times of prayer—before school, meals, at bedtime.* In particular, bedtime prayers should be unhurried and regular. This can be a great time to teach your own children about prayer and fellowship with the Father.

Self-Check

Take a few minutes to evaluate how you're fulfilling your role as a rock-solid teacher in the area of shaping lives to be like Christ. Just between you and God, rate how you're doing at teaching in this area. Spend some time in prayer asking God to help you grow in areas in which you're struggling.

Revelation of God's Glory

The priority of my teaching ministry is to reveal the glory of God through careful teaching of the Scriptures.

strongly agree   *agree*   *not sure*   *disagree*   *strongly disagree*

I don't allow other aspects of teaching—however good—to distract me from the joy of seeing my students living out God's will.

strongly agree   *agree*   *not sure*   *disagree*   *strongly disagree*

Reflection of God's Glory

I encourage times of worship in my class or in my family.

strongly agree   *agree*   *not sure*   *disagree*   *strongly disagree*

I encourage specific times of sharing in my class or family regarding times we've seen God's character being displayed through answers to prayer.

strongly agree   *agree*   *not sure*   *disagree*   *strongly disagree*

Resource for God's Glory

I recognize God's authority, work, words, name and love in my own life.

strongly agree   *agree*   *not sure*   *disagree*   *strongly disagree*

I regularly highlight God's authority, work, words, name and love in the lessons I teach.

strongly agree   *agree*   *not sure*   *disagree*   *strongly disagree*

Relationships for God's Glory

I work to build relationships with and between students that focus on evangelism, missions and life-change teaching—not around fellowship as an end in itself.

strongly agree   *agree*   *not sure*   *disagree*   *strongly disagree*

I work to teach my students about prayer and depending on the Lord.

strongly agree   *agree*   *not sure*   *disagree*   *strongly disagree*

Benediction

May the Lord who prayed for us grant us the insight to keep God's glory as our only priority. May He fill us with purpose as we serve Him through this wonderful privilege of teaching.

ROCK-SOLID TEACHER
SELF-EVALUATION

Make two photocopies of this evaluation. Use one to evaluate where you are now, and the other in six to nine months to evaluate how you've grown as a rock-solid teacher.

Teach Like Jesus!
Rock-solid teachers follow Jesus' model of proclaiming, instructing and healing.

Proclaiming

I regularly make the truths of the Scriptures known to students to allow them to hear and respond to Jesus.

strongly agree　　　agree　　　not sure　　　disagree　　　strongly disagree

I consistently declare the truths of God's Word—even the more difficult ones—so that my students desire to become more like Christ.

strongly agree　　　agree　　　not sure　　　disagree　　　strongly disagree

Instructing

I prompt interaction around Scripture during teaching times and also encourage students to search God's Word in their times of individual study.

strongly agree　　　agree　　　not sure　　　disagree　　　strongly disagree

I balance the many roles of teacher and fulfill the biblical roles.

strongly agree　　　agree　　　not sure　　　disagree　　　strongly disagree

Healing

I prepare my learners to meet the Lord Jesus Christ by meeting their needs as best I can.

strongly agree　　　agree　　　not sure　　　disagree　　　strongly disagree

I expect the Lord to accomplish life change in the hearts of my students.

strongly agree   agree   not sure   disagree   strongly disagree

Proclaim Good News
Rock-solid teachers proclaim with power and impact.

Proclaiming with Authority

If my students aren't learning, I try to change circumstances and my style so that I can gain their attention and encourage a response.

strongly agree   agree   not sure   disagree   strongly disagree

I sense a calling from God to teach truth in my class or group. As a teacher, I assume the care and feeding of my students.

strongly agree   agree   not sure   disagree   strongly disagree

I expect each student to respond to what God is teaching him or her.

strongly agree   agree   not sure   disagree   strongly disagree

Proclaiming by Presenting Your Lesson with Impact

I prepare lessons with an awareness of the strengths of my presentation (and the weaknesses) so I can proclaim truth with clarity and conviction.

strongly agree   agree   not sure   disagree   strongly disagree

I use other methods in my lecture to ensure strong learning.

strongly agree   agree   not sure   disagree   strongly disagree

Teach to Learn
Rock-solid teachers instruct students
toward obedience.

Instructing with Storytelling

With the teaching I do in my class or group, I see students learning to obey.

strongly agree   agree   not sure   disagree   strongly disagree

I use stories that lead students to seek God's will and not just to entertain.
strongly agree   agree   not sure   disagree   strongly disagree

I tell stories to capture the interest of my students by using variety and speaking with skill and passion.
strongly agree   agree   not sure   disagree   strongly disagree

Instructing with Questions
I ask questions that stimulate thinking, evaluation and life change in my students.
strongly agree   agree   not sure   disagree   strongly disagree

I use questions to get students involved in what I'm teaching.
strongly agree   agree   not sure   disagree   strongly disagree

Bring Healing
Rock-solid teachers bring healing as Jesus did—through gracious words and healthy relationships.

Speaking Gracious Words
I try to remember students' names while I'm teaching.
strongly agree   agree   not sure   disagree   strongly disagree

I look for inner qualities of character and don't make judgments based on external appearance.
strongly agree   agree   not sure   disagree   strongly disagree

I encourage others with positive statements and don't just point out areas where they need to improve.
strongly agree   agree   not sure   disagree   strongly disagree

Building Healthy Relationships
I take seriously the responsibility to build relationships with my students so that I can respond to their resistance, doubts or confusion.
strongly agree   agree   not sure   disagree   strongly disagree

I believe that it's just as important to prepare myself relationally as I do intellectually—developing a proper relationship with God, other believers and those in the world.

strongly agree   *agree*   *not sure*   *disagree*   *strongly disagree*

I find myself forgiving others even when they haven't asked for it because I know that bitterness can cause healing to evaporate.

strongly agree   *agree*   *not sure*   *disagree*   *strongly disagree*

Follow the Pattern
Rock-solid teachers use teaching patterns, experiences and activities to nurture life change.

I follow the patterns that Jesus used, not allowing the experience to be dismissed from my teaching.

strongly agree   *agree*   *not sure*   *disagree*   *strongly disagree*

I create learning experiences that have variety and meaning.

strongly agree   *agree*   *not sure*   *disagree*   *strongly disagree*

I regularly assess my students to see which method will work best in teaching them.

strongly agree   *agree*   *not sure*   *disagree*   *strongly disagree*

I'm a continual learner.

strongly agree   *agree*   *not sure*   *disagree*   *strongly disagree*

I believe in trying new ways to impact those whom I instruct.

strongly agree   *agree*   *not sure*   *disagree*   *strongly disagree*

Motivate to Learn
Rock-solid teachers are catalysts for change in the lives of their students.

I study students to know their needs, characteristics, desires and knowledge.

strongly agree   agree   not sure   disagree   strongly disagree

I prepare lessons from biblical content with a view to motivate students to learn.

strongly agree   agree   not sure   disagree   strongly disagree

My goal is to increase my observation and understanding of my students so that I can do my part to motivate them for Christ.

strongly agree   agree   not sure   disagree   strongly disagree

I regularly review motivational principles in my own life and in the lives of those I teach.

strongly agree   agree   not sure   disagree   strongly disagree

I begin my lessons with planned activity to motivate my students from where they are in life to a place where they can take a step of obedience.

strongly agree   agree   not sure   disagree   strongly disagree

I build relationships with students through activities such as encouragement, friendship, intercession and visitation.

strongly agree   agree   not sure   disagree   strongly disagree

I employ discipline and guidance in my class to motivate my students.

strongly agree   agree   not sure   disagree   strongly disagree

I seek to bring meaning to the learning situation through knowledge of my students and their learning styles.

strongly agree   agree   not sure   disagree   strongly disagree

I employ both humor and quietness in appropriate ways while teaching.

strongly agree   *agree*   *not sure*   *disagree*   *strongly disagree*

Know the Scriptures
Rock-solid teachers work to grasp the content of God's Word and help students apply it.

Know Your Students
I'm knowledgeable about my students. I've established relationships that allow me to shepherd them on a consistent basis.

strongly agree   *agree*   *not sure*   *disagree*   *strongly disagree*

I set aside time to engage in meaningful conversation and activity both in and outside of class.

strongly agree   *agree*   *not sure*   *disagree*   *strongly disagree*

I can name several of my students' friends and the impact they've had on the spiritual development of that individual.

strongly agree   *agree*   *not sure*   *disagree*   *strongly disagree*

Know the Content of Scripture
I'm aware of Scripture. I observe and interpret God's Word appropriately.

strongly agree   *agree*   *not sure*   *disagree*   *strongly disagree*

I memorize Scripture, believing the promise of Psalm 119:10-11: "I seek you with all my heart; do not let me stray from your commands. I have hidden your word in my heart that I might not sin against you."

strongly agree   *agree*   *not sure*   *disagree*   *strongly disagree*

I gather with believers of different ages and different life situations to learn the Scriptures together.

strongly agree   *agree*   *not sure*   *disagree*   *strongly disagree*

I occasionally go deeper to experience new depths of Bible study. For example, I sometimes read extended passages or a Bible commentary.

strongly agree   *agree*   *not sure*   *disagree*   *strongly disagree*

Prompt Application and Life Change

I prepare my own heart for application and expect the Holy Spirit to change me and help me grow. I know that I can't take others where I refuse to go.

strongly agree   agree   not sure   disagree   strongly disagree

I plan to lead students toward life change through using creative and specific methods that help them apply what they're learning.

strongly agree   agree   not sure   disagree   strongly disagree

I ask how my family or my students have applied the Scripture that they have studied.

strongly agree   agree   not sure   disagree   strongly disagree

Use Things, Not People
Rock-solid teachers use the teaching environment to prepare students to learn.

Enhancing Worship

I set up my classroom so that students respond to the Lord. I minimize distractions, interruptions and messy or unclean surroundings.

strongly agree   agree   not sure   disagree   strongly disagree

I use posters, bulletin boards, and other materials in the classroom to inspire reverence and thought.

strongly agree   agree   not sure   disagree   strongly disagree

I record experiences in a class journal or in drawings of what God has done with the students: answers to prayer, times of revival, memories of worship times, and so forth.

strongly agree   agree   not sure   disagree   strongly disagree

Enhancing Learning

I use the environment to enhance learning through a healing climate, available resources and appropriate preparation.

strongly agree   agree   not sure   disagree   strongly disagree

I bring informality into learning times by using real-life examples and activities.

strongly agree   agree   not sure   disagree   strongly disagree

Variety in schedule and availability are a part of my teaching.

strongly agree   agree   not sure   disagree   strongly disagree

Enhancing Fellowship

I use the learning environment to enhance fellowship by making our classroom settings inviting.

strongly agree   agree   not sure   disagree   strongly disagree

I make sure that temperature, lighting and seating are comfortable and appropriate.

strongly agree   agree   not sure   disagree   strongly disagree

I sometimes provide refreshments to encourage fellowship in the group.

strongly agree   agree   not sure   disagree   strongly disagree

Enhancing Service

I work with others in our church to make sure we provide opportunities for service by not being too stiff and rigid about our buildings.

strongly agree   agree   not sure   disagree   strongly disagree

I provide places and times to pray for those who serve our church, for missionaries, and for other Christian workers sent out from our church.

strongly agree   agree   not sure   disagree   strongly disagree

I occasionally plan a class or family project to work on together: putting together holiday food baskets, cleaning houses or raking yards, making Angel Tree projects for prisoners, doing special visitations for those who are sick, participating in evangelism events.

strongly agree   agree   not sure   disagree   strongly disagree

Keep the Main Thing the Main Thing
Rock-solid teachers shape
lives to be like Christ.

Revelation of God's Glory

The priority of my teaching ministry is to reveal the glory of God through careful teaching of the Scriptures.

strongly agree   agree   not sure   disagree   strongly disagree

I don't allow other aspects of teaching—however good—to distract me from the joy of seeing my students living out God's will.

strongly agree   agree   not sure   disagree   strongly disagree

Reflection of God's Glory

I encourage times of worship in my class or in my family.

strongly agree   agree   not sure   disagree   strongly disagree

I encourage specific times of sharing in my class or family regarding times we've seen God's character being displayed through answers to prayer.

strongly agree   agree   not sure   disagree   strongly disagree

Resource for God's Glory

I recognize God's authority, work, words, name and love in my own life.

strongly agree   agree   not sure   disagree   strongly disagree

I regularly highlight God's authority, work, words, name and love in the lessons I teach.

strongly agree   agree   not sure   disagree   strongly disagree

Relationships for God's Glory

I work to build relationships with and between students that focus on evangelism, missions and life-change teaching—not around fellowship as an end in itself.

strongly agree   agree   not sure   disagree   strongly disagree

I work to teach my students about prayer and depending on the Lord.
strongly agree   *agree*   *not sure*   *disagree*   *strongly disagree*

ENDNOTES

Chapter 1: Teach Like Jesus!

1. Roy B. Zuck, *Spirit-Filled Teaching: The Holy Spirit in Your Teaching* (Wheaton, IL: Scripture Press, 1963), p. 125.
2. Bruce Wilkinson, *The Seven Laws of the Learner: How to Teach Almost Anything to Practically Anyone* (Sisters, OR: Multnomah Press, 1992), p. 41.
3. W. E. Vine, *An Expository Dictionary of New Testament Words* (Old Tappan, NJ: Fleming H. Revell, 1966), p. 201.
4. For a great resource that can help you share the gospel simply with children, see chapter 7 of Larry Fowler, *Rock-Solid Kids: Giving Kids a Biblical Foundation for Life* (Ventura, CA: Gospel Light, 2005).

Chapter 2: Proclaim Good News

1. Coolie Verner and Gary Dickinson, "The Lecture: An Analysis and Review of Research," *Adult Education Quarterly* (1967), v. 17, no. 2, p. 90.

Chapter 3: Teach to Learn

1. Anita Woolfolk, ed., *Educational Psychology, 8th edition* (Boston, MA: Allyn and Bacon, 2001), p. 254.
2. *Gospel Light's Children's Ministry Smart Pages, Grades 1-6* (Ventura, CA: Gospel Light, 2004), pp. 221-222.
3. James M. Cooper, ed., *Classroom Teaching Skills, 6th edition* (Boston, MA: Houghton Mifflin Company, 1999), p. 106.
4. William R. Yount, *Created to Learn* (Nashville, TN: Broadman and Holman Publishers, 1996), p. 304.
5. Henrietta C. Mears, *What the Bible Is All About, 2nd revised edition* (Ventura, CA: Regal Books, 1997), pages 676-677.
6. Wes Haystead, *Bible 101* (Cincinnati, OH: Standard Publishing, 1997).

Chapter 4: Bring Healing

1. Ivy Beckwith, *Postmodern Children's Ministry: Ministry to Children in the 21st Century* (Grand Rapids, MI: Zondervan, 2004), pp. 80-95.
2. Doug Fields, "Relational Basics, How to Develop Relationships with Kids," *Youthworker Journal*, March/April, 2002, p. 22.
3. Rorheim Institute, *Shepherding Parents* (Streamwood, IL: Rorheim Institute, Awana Clubs International, 2006).
4. Larry Fowler, *Rock-Solid Kids* (Ventura, CA: Gospel Light Publications, 2004), pp. 101-130.

Chapter 5: Follow the Pattern

1. Bruce H. Wilkinson, *The Seven Laws of the Learner* (Atlanta, GA: Walk Thru the Bible Ministries, 1988), pp. 52-53.

2. These categories are parallel to descriptions in: Stephen L. Yelon, *Powerful Principles of Instruction* (White Plains, NY: Longman Publishing, 1996), pp. 204-208.

3. Barbara Bolton, *How to Do Bible Learning Activities, Book 2* (Ventura, CA: Gospel Light, 1984), p. 9.

4. Jerome W. Berryman, *Godly Play: An Imaginative Approach to Religious Education* (Minneapolis, MN: Augsburg, 1991), n.p.

5. *Children's Ministry Smart Pages, Grades 1-6* (Ventura, CA: Gospel Light, 2004), pp. 147-148.

6. Rorheim Institute, *Shepherding Parents* (Streamwood, IL: Rorheim Institute, Awana Clubs International, 2005), pp. 40-41.

Chapter 6: Motivate to Learn

1. Anita Woolfolk, ed., *Educational Psychology, 8th edition* (Boston, MA: Allyn and Bacon, 2001), pp. 375-376.

2. Gregory C. Carlson, *Understanding Teaching; Effective Biblical Teaching for the 21st Century, Instructional Resource Pack* (Wheaton, IL: Evangelical Training Association, 1998), p. 55.

3. Marlene LeFever, *Learning Styles: Reaching Everyone God Gave You to Teach* (Colorado Springs, CO: Cook Communications, 1995), pp. 23-35.

4. Lawrence O. Richards and Gary J. Bredfeldt, *Creative Bible Teaching* (Chicago: Moody Press, 1998), p. 239.

5. Stephen L. Yelon, *Powerful Principles of Instruction* (White Plains, NY: Longman Publishing, 1996), p. 281.

6. Lawrence O. Richards, *Expository Dictionary of Bible Words* (Grand Rapids, MI: Zondervan Publishing House, 1985), p. 605.

7. Woolfolk, *Educational Psychology, 8th edition,* p. 368.

8. *How to Teach Kids Using Guided Conversation (Grades 1-6)* (Ventura, CA: Gospel Light, 1993), video notes, p. 3.

Chapter 7: Know the Scriptures

1. Bruce Wilkinson, *The Seven Laws of the Learner: How to Teach Almost Anything to Practically Anyone!* (Sisters, OR: Multnomah Press, 1992), p. 126.

2. Howard Hendricks and William D. Hendricks, *Living by the Book* (Chicago: Moody Press, 1991), p. 286.

3. Dave Veerman, *How to Apply the Bible* (Wheaton, IL: Tyndale House Publishers, 1993), p. 15.

4. Wes and Sheryl Haystead, *How to Have a Great Sunday School: Sunday School Standards for All Age Groups* (Ventura, CA: Gospel Light, 2000), pp. 42-43.

5. Hans Finzel, *Observe, Interpret, Apply: How to Study the Bible Inductively* (Wheaton, IL: Victor Books, 1994), p. 70.

6. What's a Family Together Sunday School class? In my view, we need a revolution in Sunday School structure. Check out Rorheim Institute's *Shepherding Parents* (Streamwood, IL: Rorheim Institute, Awana Clubs International, 2005); Charles Sell's *Family Ministry, 2nd edition* (Grand Rapids, MI: Zondervan, 1995); Ben Freudenburg and Rick Lawrence's *The Family Friendly Church* (Loveland, CO: Vital Books, Group Publishing, 1998); Familywise's *2-52 Basics: Growing in Wisdom, Faith and Relationships* (http://www.252basics.com/); North Point Community Church's *Kidstuf* (Alpharetta, GA, http://kidstuf.com/).

Chapter 8: Use Things, Not People

1. One of my favorites is *Gospel Light's Children's Ministry Smart Pages, Grades 1-6* (Ventura, CA: Gospel Light, 2004).
2. See Gregory C. Carlson, *Understanding Teaching Instructional Resource Pak* (Wheaton, IL: Evangelical Training Association, 1998), chapter 7.
3. Wes and Sheryl Haystead, *How to Have a Great Sunday School: Sunday School Standards for All Age Groups* (Ventura, CA: Gospel Light, 2000). Another classic book is: Lowell E. Brown, *Sunday School Standards; A Guide for Measuring and Achieving Sunday School Success* (Ventura, CA: Gospel Light Publications, 1980, 1996).
4. Ginny Olson, Diane Elliot and Mike Work, *Youth Ministry Management Tools* (Grand Rapids, MI: Zondervan, 2001), pp. 310-311.
5. The Navigators, *Topical Bible Memory System* (Colorado Springs, CO: NavPress, 2005).
6. *The Discipleship Journal* online Bible Reading Plan, NavPress. http://www.navpress.com/Magazines/DiscipleshipJournal/OriginalBibleReadingPlan/.

Chapter 9: Keep the Main Thing the Main Thing

1. Reggie McNeal, *The Present Future; Six Tough Questions for the Church* (San Francisco: Jossey-Bass, 2003), pp. xvi-xvii.
2. Tommy Walker, "He Knows My Name" (Nashville: Doulos Publishing, 1997), from *More Songs for Praise and Worship 2* (Waco, TX: Word, 2002), song #109.
3. Wes and Sheryl Haystead, *Teaching Your Child About God* (Ventura, CA: Gospel Light, 1995), pp. 90-91.
4. Ibid.
5. *PrayKids!* online resource, NavPress. http://www.navpress.com/Magazines/PrayKids/.
6. Esther Ilnisky, *Let the Children Pray* (Ventura, CA: Gospel Light, 2000).

BIBLIOGRAPHY

General Teaching Tools

Carlson, Gregory C. *Understanding Teaching Effective Biblical Teaching for the 21st Century*. Wheaton, IL: Evangelical Training Association, 1998.

Thigpen, Jonathan, ed. *Teaching Techniques*. Wheaton, IL: Evangelical Training Association, 2001.

These are two fine training tools from an experienced training group that enable teachers who teach any age group to prepare, teach and/or use Bible lessons.

Gregory, John Milton. *The Seven Laws of Teaching, Revised Edition*. Grand Rapids, MI: Baker Books, 2003. This classic never wears out. Principles of teaching, time-tested.

Haystead, Wes and Sheryl. *How to Have a Great Sunday School: Sunday School Standards for All Age Groups*. Ventura, CA: Gospel Light, 2000. An update of the great standards for administrating a great Sunday School.

Richards, Lawrence O. and Gary J. Bredfeldt, *Creative Bible Teaching*. Chicago: Moody Press, 1998. The "Hook, Book, Look, Took" teaching outline is used by many teachers to give a biblical pattern to their teaching.

Wilkinson, Bruce. *The Seven Laws of the Learner: How to Teach Almost Anything to Practically Anyone!* Sisters, OR: Multnomah Publishers, 1992. A creative book updating the laws of teaching.

Woolfolk, Anita, ed. *Educational Psychology, eighth edition*. Boston, MA: Allyn and Bacon, 2001. A sound educational psychology textbook for the more serious reader.

Yelon, Stephen L., *Powerful Principles of Instruction*. White Plains, NY: Longman Publishing, 1996. A fine educational psychology text written for school teachers.

Children's Teaching Tools

Fowler, Larry. *Rock-Solid Kids*. Ventura, CA: Gospel Light, 2004. Outlines eight standards for children's ministry in the local church.

Gospel Light's Children's Ministry Smart Pages, Grades 1-6. Ventura, CA: Gospel Light, 2004. One of a number of fine resources from the publisher that leads the way in Bible learning activities.

Haystead, Wes and Sheryl. *Teaching Your Child About God*. Ventura, CA: Gospel Light, 1995. Especially good for younger children.

Youth Teaching Tools

Habermas, Ron. *Teaching for Reconciliation*. Eugene, OR: Wipf and Stock Publishers, 2001. While this comprehensive book deals with the teaching of all age groups, I especially like the youth-teaching material.

Olson, Ginny, Diane Elliot and Mike Work. *Youth Ministry Management Tools*. Grand Rapids, MI: Zondervan Publishing House, 2001. A great administrative tool for establishing a teaching ministry.

Schultz, Thom and Joani. *Do It! Active Learning in Youth Ministry*. Loveland, CO: Group Publishing, 2000. Provides a good variety of methods for teaching youth from two of the more creative teachers in the country.

Adult Teaching Tools

LeFever, Marlene. *Learning Styles: Reaching Everyone God Gave You to Teach*. Colorado Springs, CO: Cook Communications, 1995. Marlene brings practical skills to the task of teaching. A masterful book to assist teachers in holistic teaching. I put this under "adults," but it has applications for all levels.

Silberman, Mel. *101 Ways to Make Training Active, 2nd edition*. San Francisco, CA: John Wiley and Sons, Inc., 2005. A super tool for trainers and teachers. One of the best resources for creativity you can find.

Family Teaching Tools

Freudenburg, Ben, and Rick Lawrence. *The Family Friendly Church*. Loveland, CO: Vital Books, Group Publishing, 1998.

Rorheim Institute. *Shepherding Parents*. Streamwood, IL: Rorheim Institute, a department of Awana Clubs International, 2005. A training seminar for church leaders to equip parents to evangelize and disciple their kids.

Weaver, Kirk. *Family Time CD-ROM Curriculum*. Littleton, CO: Family Time Training, 2006. The mission of Family Time Training is to train families to teach children Christian principles and values in the home.

Raise Your Children to Love Jesus

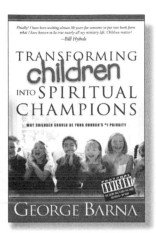
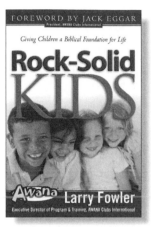
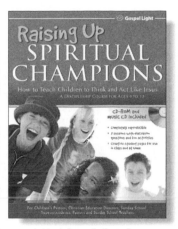
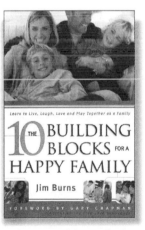
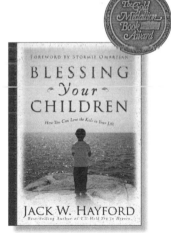
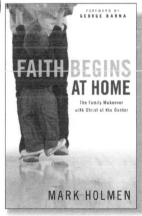